SCARS

Poems & Short Stories About Mental Health and Healing

Compiled and Edited by
Kathy Chaffin Gerstorff & Stacy Savage

ISBN: 9798379307172

Dedication

This book is dedicated to the loved ones we have lost to mental illness.

Acknowledgments

Thank you SCARS anthology contributing authors for sharing your poems and stories to bring this project to life!

Big Sal, Bryan Franco, Chuck Kellum, Clara Klein, Clay Octobre, Colleen Wells, D.A. Carns, Diana Humphrey, EB Hills, Elizabeth Cox, Isabella St. Kim, Jason Bayliss, Jessica Oakwood, John Ganshaw, Julie A. Dickson, Karuna Mistry, Kathy Chaffin Gerstorff, Leland Gamson, Lori Goss-Reaves, Marcia Durant, Marj O'Neill-Butler, Michael Strosahl, Mikayla Cyr, Ndaba Sibanda, Noel Arzola, Pratibha Savani, Rachel Leitch, Sarfraz Ahmed, Stacy Savage, Stephanie Daich, Teresa Keefer, Terra Chism, William Lewis, and Zaneta Varnado Johns

Special thanks to SCARS book launch sponsor, Minnetrista Museum & Gardens.

Table of Contents

Content Warning

Potentially Sensitive Content

This book mentions issues that may be sensitive or triggering. Topics may include, but are not limited to, child abuse, sexual assault, domestic violence, self-harm, suicide, eating disorders, death, miscarriages, abortions, mental illness, profanity, etc. The content warning is not intended to censor material, rather to enable trauma survivors to be prepared to skip triggering content and process information under controlled conditions. Your mental health and safety are of utmost importance.

Introduction

We never know how the dots will connect from the experiences of our lives. How can we know what we survive can one day be used to help others? It makes me grateful to have survived my childhood trauma of physical, mental, verbal, sexual abuse, and two suicide attempts. I would have much rather had a father who loved and protected me than a stepfather whose mental illness and abuse towards his family caused years of needless PTSD, addiction, anxiety, and mistrust. If he would have gotten help, perhaps he would have stopped the generational abuse.

After escaping the abuse, I had a choice to make. I could remain a victim and let the anger consume me or it could stop with me. I got the help I needed in a way that healed my scarred soul - through books, workshops, and seminars. (See the Resources page for a list.) This was long before the Internet made information instantly available. Writing and music also helped me process my emotions so I didn't keep them all bottled up and implode.

My wish is for you to find what helps you heal and leave a legacy of love for future generations. It's a tall order, but if you're reading this book, you have what it takes to overcome obstacles and lead a good life.

Thank you for purchasing SCARS and helping mental health organizations continue their mission of providing hope to those walking through the fire. You made a difference today. May your thoughtfulness and generosity multiply beyond your wildest imagination! I hope the poems and stories help you on your healing journey.

To the contributing authors, I can't thank you enough for being vulnerable in sharing your stories and poetry. You are proof that we can come out stronger on the other side of trauma and mental health issues. Bless you. Thank you!

Kathy Chaffin Gerstorff,
SCARS Publishing Author
& Victorious Survivor

Forever Fraud Philanthropists *by Big Sal*

Hella drama as I suffer if it lives for smashing stone, Tell my mama that I love her and my kids that daddy's home, Lift a fist when laughs are gone from a mime's fake cup of facts, It's a risk to have me grown with my mind made up like masks, As the time takes us to task and we bake the food to best say - That the blind make drugs in class and we make it through the next day, Facing 401s to go 'round, With a halberd that we bring home, Raising moral funds to cope now, It's a sellsword in the sea foam.

~~~

Stay as psycho east of county as the feds propose the worst, May survival reap its bounty on the heads of those it cursed, Pack the cut, soak it in absinthe, and the actresses are blonde, Cracking up open the lapis when the lattices are strong, My life was messy in its season like I's reading wiki gumbo, My wife had left me then for Steven and my Eden quickly crumbled, Kiss thy evening and she's supple with my pride as asters die, If I'm weeping as we'd rumble and I'd try to ask her why.

~~~

A clown creeps in up the sunset with a gum stick in the rules, I now keep it but a hundred as I run it like the jewels, If I'm damn sure but a soldier with my fam here staying numb, As I asked her for my closure and she sat there playing dumb, Rhyme like rappers as I enter in a separate sewer lifeless, I'm a bastard with a temper but I'd never do her like this, Be Adonis, hence she wept in the scene's dead lover's eyes, She had promised since we met but my dreams said otherwise, Stand the deep end of her thighs if she wears bush like a camo, And to bleed men under skies like a werewolf or I'm Rambo, Shift the feeling for the objects like a village that is vetted, If the healing is a process and it kills us if we let it.

Seppuku in Summertime *by Big Sal*

A written week to walk free from the weighted knife like Nestlé,
I sit and weep as softly as the day my wife had left me,
Fear the rebel's lively brother as he sticks to sake coffee,
Pierce the nettle/ivy cover with a wicked wakizashi,
Drift and tug the waters nightly with this poem aptly theirs,
Kiss and hug my daughters tightly as I show 'em Daddy cares,
Find the wrong sum leads to hating on the rest then when you're dumb,
I'm the shotgun preacher waiting on the steps and with a gun,
Weapons show the shots ahead with the sacred tongues of lore,
Let 'em know their gods are dead when I take their sons to war.
~~~
Taste the land and dawn the whole sea as the leaves drown in the
brooks, Place my hand upon an oak tree as I bleed out in my books,
Crush the matrix like a dug dune in the healer's darkest evening,
Push the pages to my gut wound as you feel my heart is beating,
Give us weapons and the gas kegs as we show the fist and fast glove,
Live as legends on their last legs as we blow a kiss to past love,
Cash-in cards still help the mamas if the time it waits for this,
As my scars will melt katanas and the finest blades of bliss.
~~~
Dealing bones like winter soldiers with the smiles of a best friend,
Building homes as cinders smolder in the piles that we left them,
It's a dead tone held in view like an iPhone in thy pocket,
With the whetstone Belgian Blue and the grindstone by the rocket,
So consigners sew the liners with the Roanoke and diver,
Oppenheimer opened time here with a broken bro kin timer,
Wet the dirt bag on a rock in a universe to be,
Setting Earth back on a clock that a doomsday's sure to see,
Coals and crofts that will be sit-ins for the fancy and their skin tone,
Souls aloft in silky linens as they're dancing on the brimstone,
Going broke and east where Death is in a village house though lonely,
Blowing smoke to ease their stresses as I kill myself so slowly.

Color Me Scars *by Big Sal*

Ask a couple and a wife if they've heard of perfect wisdom,
As I struggle and I strive for a nurtured nervous system,
Find I'm calm as I squeeze on the all-brown sticks and more,
I'm a bomb in the breeze as the fallout drifts to shore,
Go to bat and fight the bunts of advice on a sword's swing,
So, I sat and cried for months when my wife then divorced me,
Bottles sell by the pint, such is luck for the bland,
All is well, I am fine, suck it up, you're a champ!
(Woefully wipes tears and [SNIFFLES])
Drift away with every raft if it's a tad stuck to pack blades,
It's okay to let me have it when I'm back up on that stage,
So, we same folks know to quit so the bliss will last for all those,
Throw tomatoes; throw your shit; throw the piss you stash in bottles,
Build with dark doubt for the light as it whizzed into the shore,
Spill my heart out on this mic as it drips onto the floor,
Get my wrath to rhyme in vengeance for the czars I lull to drink,
Yet I have to find acceptance in the scars I color pink.
~~~
Who's to think the wells are deep down the same cut of the isle?
Used to drink myself to sleep, now I wake up with a smile,
Bet the danger wasn't early in the temples with the hell glow,
Yet the anger doesn't serve me and assembles in a salvo,
Climb to camp through hardships prying on a Hennessey sud or sink,
I'm a tattoo artist dying with his enemy's blood for ink.
~~~
Ever since the night I met her I'm a soldier for her heart,
Reminisce when I'd protect her and I'd hold her in the dark,
Due to pain I come to crumble with the humble where the dead sleep,
Through the rain and thunder rumbles as we'd tumble near the
bedsheet, Wow, the end it sees is ours in the ashes and my urn,
Now the memories are scars and the badges that I've earned,

To then save me (now I weep) from the coldness of the crypts,
You can lay me down to sleep with her lotus on my lips.

I Never Understood What The Feathers Were For
by Bryan Franco

When I was young, I was shy and awkward.
I had learning and motor disabilities.
I was uncoordinated and unathletic.
It wasn't uncommon for other kids
to tar and feather me with their words
with the goal of causing permanent scars.
Along the way, I became friends with other kids
who had been tarred and feathered themselves.
As we got older, we became immune to tar
due to all the buildup over the years which
eventually chipped away from our identities
and what was underneath wasn't scars
but a glow of fuck youism because we knew
the bullies would learn they were bullies
when their kids became bullies because they could
never erase being a bully from their identities.

The Land of the Glass Cattails *by Bryan Franco*

For it has been told, a drunken angel fell to earth and
landed in a muddy marsh filled with cattails.
The marsh transformed: mud turned to silky sugar white sand;
cattails turned to glass. There was no more darkness or rain.
Light refracted through the cattails producing little pieces of
broken rainbows that could cure a lost soul of life's ills.

Before you broke the glass cattails, you googled
how to snap a human soul in half like a twig.
You were wearing boots made for tromping through marshes
and snapping cattails like twigs.

When you broke the glass cattails, you made a decision
to break me as if I was crisp autumn leaves beneath your feet.
You had decided you were a giant and I was
Jack come to pillage your castle.

The day after you broke the glass cattails,
you woke wearing those boots.
They were fused to your feet, words, actions, and attitude.

When you left the castle, your boots and you
bought an axe to chop down a beanstalk.
You needed to destroy my world and bring
me down to your level, but I live in a different world
where beanstalks grow beans and castles in the sky are fiction.
I landed on my own two feet and walked away
with more than a few bumps, bruises, scrapes, and scars.

I learned abusers are hunters and abused people often
happen to be in the wrong place at the wrong time
when a hunter is out sniffing for new prey.

What you never learned was that a person
can't break someone else's soul, only their own.

As long as you choose to wear those boots,
you'll be breaking off bits and pieces of your soul
every day for the rest of your life.

When You Don't Know All Your Words Are Tattooed on Your Face *by Bryan Franco*

You told me my house was made of straw
and you were the big bad wolf.
Your words were hurricane-force winds
that blew my house down.
I grew my next crop of hay in red clay
so, my next home could resist you.

Then your words were made of fire
and my charred skin chipped away
revealing a leathery elephant hide
that was heat and flame proof.

So, you ordered your words
to spit acid in my face.
but the tears that rolled over
the hardened scars on my cheeks
learned to repel you.

All your words,
even when you try to be nice,
are laced with ruinous disdain,
but when you speak at others,
you are actually talking to yourself.

Wind has permanently mussed
your stylish coif,
leaving you unkempt-looking.

Fire has singed your eyebrows,
permeating your warped conscience
with the putrid aroma
of burnt human hair.
All that acid you consumed
has etched nooks and crannies
into your soul
that can only be filled with regret.

Welcome to the mirror
you have chosen to live in.

The Person That You Are *by Chuck Kellum*

You don't always have to be
  the brightest shining star;
And when you heal, you can reveal
  that there is still a scar.
The pain you feel is very real
  and proves that life is hard.
It is okay
For you to be
The person that you are.

The person that you are
  includes the one you've been.
The good and bad, the glad and sad,
  are all contained within.
Let go of what has harmed you,
  and cherish what's been good;
And at long last, just let the past
  remain there as it should.

Accept the love that you receive
  from those who hold you dear,
And know they want to help you through
  all times of doubt and fear.
Allow them to be close to you,
  no matter how near or far.
And let them know,
Just let it show,
The person that you are.

Now as you move ahead with life,
  no matter what goes wrong –
Please never be afraid to laugh,

or to sing a sad, sad song.
Work to get the things you need,
   and you will not be poor.
With love and faith
Give of yourself
The person that you are.

Once, Out In The Rain *by Chuck Kellum*

Once, out in the rain
I sat --
Crying.

Hunched, shivering,
Bedraggled, drenched . . .
There in a downpour
The careful arrangement of my life
Now drowned.

Tilting back,
I reached up,
Sobbing,
Beseeching,
Hoping,
For deliverance,
Or transformation, --
Or *something* . . .

But nothing
Came down
But the raindrops

And more tears.

* * *

After the rain had gone
I remained
Awhile, alone,
Quiet and still

In a soggy, muddied puddle --
Waiting, waiting,
Waiting . . .

Then, as the clouds drifted off
And the sun's warmth
                gently returned,

I, slowly,
Rose
And walked away.

Living *by Chuck Kellum*

In honor of my Dad

The stroke didn't stop him.
Before long, he was walking again
With a cane, but not a walker.

Then came the crash, him
Suspended upside down in the small, crumpled pickup,
Banged up, brain bleeding in several places,
Until the rescuers arrived to get him free --
An eternity suffered alone
That he cannot remember.

And once again, at 90, he must strive
To relearn the basics
Of upright movement
That as a toddler long ago,
And without even realizing it then,
He had quickly discovered is
One of our most natural acts
Of freedom.

With that freedom he had become quite athletic
In his youth, unusually tall and excelling
In basketball – as a record-setting scorer,
And baseball – although unable or unwilling
         to advance past playing semi-pro.

Now even the simplest movements of feet and legs
Can be quite tedious when working at walking,
         And often frustrating,
                  And sometimes discouraging.

And yet, as I watch him
Rise slowly from the wheelchair, I'm sure,
Despite the limitations of his current condition,
He is still ready
To shoot that soft jumper from the baseline
Or bound, outstretched and straining,
To field the hard grounder hit to his right.

The Dreams of a Woman or Man *by Chuck Kellum*

The wind will beat against my face
        on days when I am tired;
My bones will ache,
My spirits fade . . .
The storm will drown the fire.

I'll fall asleep
        and not know when
I'll rise to meet the sun,
And dreams will guide me once again
To a place where I belong.

"Fear not,"
My soul will say to me,
"For Life is not a plan;
And what goes wrong
Cannot belong
To the dreams of a woman or man."

With a mind refreshed
And a body strong,
Travail won't hinder me;
The storm will pass,
I'll carry on:

Into another day.

Death by Depression *by Clara Klein*

It is a loss of light that kills.
All living things need light to live.
The curtain comes down,
Sometimes slowly and imperceptible,
Other times dropped like a boom.
It is a choking.
Needing air to live,
I can no longer breathe it in.........
The fog that surrounds me is poison.
It is a desiccation.
Needing water to function,
There is nothing good that flows in
Or washes over.
It is an implosion.
From wearying silence
To raucous drums in the brain,
The reverberations shatter the calm.
It is a stunting.
Failure to thrive.
No reason, no room,
No fertilizer, no growth.
No more.

A Day Off from Depression *by Clara Klein*

I pray for days like this.
For the life spirit to fill me up,
Make me alive again.
I want to feel again.
I've been numb and immobile,
paralyzed by the fear of living.
This spirit in me makes me move.
It is life ecstatic.
I feel like I can jump up into the universe.
My arms reach out as if to grasp it.
I long for it to pull me up.
Pull me out of my darkness!
And I am full of thanks
For things I cannot do alone.
It is a brief interlude –
Afterwards I ache and am fatigued.
Rest now, the universe says.

Old Man Depression *by Clara Klein*

Old Man Depression

Is here again

This time with a vengeance

Although there is no logic

To his presence

He is pervasive

He is beating me down

Help me somebody help me

Get out of his binds

The trappings are weighing me down

I don't want to be here

Locked in this stronghold

Please set me free

And let me be!

Mary O Margaret *by Clay Octobre*

Mary O Margaret, what a story to tell,

Flawed, imperfect, sometimes scary as well.

Five-foot nothing and around eight and a half stone,

But when I was a boy, I felt she could change the world alone.

Athletic, funny, and amazing to see,

Groundbreaking, mold making, and unique was she.

A deer slayer, card player, hog rider, and mechanic too.

As I live and breathe, I thought there was nothing she couldn't do.

On my wall is a seventy-year-old drawing she made,

Bordered in green and slightly grayed.

A bear, holding two flags, in a navy suit.

When I look at it, I swear, I hear the horn toot.

The drawing's corners and edges have worn down,

But the spirit of the artist is as clear as the horn's sound.

For on the lower left corner the signature declares it clear,

Mary "The Artist" Mains was here!

The funny thing is, my heart is the same,

For it has been blessed to be signed with the artist's name.

Just like the parchment, which hangs on my wall,

Mary O Margaret was here, it shouts to one and all.

Little things I do and little things that I say,

Remind me of you each-and-every day.

My heart breaks, for I fear the day,

When, just like us all, Mary O Margaret must go away.

But I will remember the amazing things I have watched you do.

I will remember the heartaches and pain you have suffered through.

The scars caused by the loss of Dad and Louise, come to mind.

The world we live in is often so very-very unkind,

But a promise was made before Mary "the Artist" was here.

A promise by God through his son, which we hold dear.

At Isaiah 25:8 Jehovah God says he will remove tears from all faces.

This means from all people, all races, and from all places.

So, if the inevitable should come before that day,

I know that, through Jesus, the stone will be rolled away.

And just like in John eleven Jesus will shout,

Mary "The Artist" Mains it's time to come out!

Then this world's system, which has been so unkind,

Will be done away with and be put out of mind.

A blessing from God, true peace we will see.

For Mary Margaret Mains will be alive and free.

Her blue eyes sparkling for all the world to see.

Through God's Son, Jesus, we will have the chance,

To run, to race, play ball, or dance.

Mary O Margaret I am proud to be your son.

I am thankful for all Mary Margaret Mains has done.

Mary O Margaret, WHAT A STORY TO TELL,

Flawed, imperfect, sometimes scary, and ALWAYS loved as well.

Vengeance *by Clay Octobre*

Vengeance, what a sad thing!

Have you ever wondered why God said, "Vengeance is mine; I will repay?" I have. As a young boy, I looked around and could not understand why so many people suffered so much. I saw poverty, abuse, addiction, and more. Why wasn't anyone doing anything to stop it?

Families, who were supposed to love each other, couldn't be in the same room. The same circumstance existed between my dad and oldest brother, Delano. They fought constantly. They argued over everything. The weather, sports, relationships, and the color of red.

It seemed to me; Delano was always looking for ways to take shots at dad. It didn't matter that dad always allowed Delano to return home after he managed to screw up and end up homeless. He never thanked dad for getting up in the middle of the night to drive hours to get him out of a jam and then go to work with no sleep. I was certain Delano hated Dad.

I resented Delano for the way he disrespected dad. Dad was my hero. Please don't misunderstand me. Dad wasn't perfect. He had flaws, but he was a good man. So, I planned to grow up, get strong and repay Delano for his lack of respect for dad. Vengeance.

One thing I never understood was why dad allowed Delano to speak to him in the manner he did. Dad was a powerful man. I don't write these words from the perspective of a naive youth.
I write this because he was simply powerful. One example of this is an incident between dad and a man a foot taller than dad and forty years younger. At the time I was around thirty and dad was nearing seventy.

I was reaching for the door at a Hill's Department store. When a man burst through the door, with fear in his eyes as if his life was hanging in the balance. He was handsome, tall, athletic, and pale white, except for the clear red handprint across the right side of his face. The paw print was huge and well defined. As I turned back to the door, out came my dad.

Dad ran past me and was yelling at the pale rider. Dad's intentions were clear. He felt the man needed a matching blow to even out the color. I grabbed dad by the arm and ducked. I knew a slap would follow; he hadn't recognized me yet. Once dad, with my help, got himself under control. I learned the entire story.

Dad was in line waiting to pay for his purchase. The young man, in front of him, was trying to steal money from the cashier, by asking for change and quick-talking the young lady. Dad recognized the scam and told the young lady, "Close your drawer! This punk is trying to steal from you!"

The man then responded, to dear OLD dad, "Shut up old man! This ain't your business!"

According to the cashier and everyone in line. Dad responded with a lightning quick open handed slap. The slap flipped the con artist one hundred and eighty degrees off his feet, causing his head to strike the floor. They said the slap sounded like a wet rag slapping a countertop and that the con artist's feet were running before he got them back on the floor. I am not sure the young man ever stopped running.

The question then, why did dad allow Delano such room for error? My brother had disappeared again. This was his modus operandi. While he was gone for about ten years, I grew up and grew strong, nothing like dad. My need for vengeance had diminished.

I had been through the horrible teen years and had a few disagreements with dad. Remember, he wasn't perfect, neither am I.

Delano returned home and soon reminded me of his disdain for our dad. I wasn't the young boy who wanted to beat him to a pulp. I was however the young man who decided to give him an extra thump during football games for dad.

In time, Delano and I became close. We built a brotherly relationship, one that mattered. We would often have coffee and breakfast together and talk about this and that. The topics varied, most of which included sports, women, and his ex-wives. One breakfast however was different. Delano was serious and brooding. His face showed real emotions, not just his normal scowl.

"What's wrong brother?" I asked.

"How well do you know dad?" He asked as he leaned forward. There it was again. The disdain he had for our dad. We have the same father, different mothers, and different views of the same dad. I controlled my response and hoped I would learn where this anger came from.

"I think I know him well. Why? What's up?"

"Do you know we had another brother, Bob Edwin? Did you know he died young?" He responded as he made certain we maintained eye contact.

In my mind, I thought of course I know we had another brother and he died young. What a silly question. I responded differently.
"Yes, I know about Bob Edwin. I know he died young, but not much more than that. Dad rarely spoke about him."

Delano slipped a copy of a state form, printed sideways on the paper.

"Read This!" He insisted.

I gleaned the information from the copy. It was a simple document, heartless and cold. The document listed all the pertinent information: name, date of birth, height, weight, and other vitals. The most alarming detail stopped me in my tracks. Cause of death: Malnutrition.

Delano fidgeted in his seat as I read the document. He anxiously awaited a response, as I read and reread Father: Mother: and Cause of Death: Malnutrition.

"What do you think of our dad now?! As he pointed to the cause of death.

"He abandoned our brother and let him starve to death! He left mom and me and let Bob starve to death! Our brother! What do you think of our dad now!"

He knew how much I held dad in high regard. My response was true. "I don't know what to think?"

The dad I knew didn't add up to the evidence Delano was forcing me to see. For over thirty years I saw a man who fed people he didn't like. A man who would drop off fifty pounds of food on my porch, just to make sure me and my family could eat. A man who would let family and strangers stay with him when they were down on their luck. Family like Delano.

"You think our dad is a good man. Does a good man leave his son to starve? Does that sound like a good man?" Delano growled.
Delano's face was painted with anger and feelings of betrayal. Those emotions were plain to see. There was another emotion which hid in

the shadows of his face. An emotion which only appeared when Delano would pause from his ranting and catch his breath. I could see guilt. Here in plain view was the reason for his anger. The scar he had been digging at for years. The injury ran deep. His scar ran through his mind and soul like thread stitched to broken cloth.

It had him trapped in the past with no way out.

Delano and I sat for hours as he pulled at the thread. Each tug would remind him of another mistake our dad had made. Another transgression he stored on his mind, like microfilm stored in an old library.

"How did you find this out?" I asked.

He spoke to me of his aunt, on his mother's side. After the death of Bob Edwin, Delano went to live with his aunt and uncle.
"Delano." I paused. "Have you ever talked to your mother about this?"

"No. I haven't spoken with my mother in twenty years."

It was clear, by his tone, he never intended to speak with her again. Our morning breakfast and coffee ended way past lunch. Delano was angry with me because I wouldn't write off our dad. There was no denying the evidence which Delano had given me nor was there anyway to deny the past three decades of my dad's behavior. The actions of an ornery old man with a big heart.

Sadly, my brother disappeared out of my life again. This time was for good. The last thing he said to me was, "I don't need any of you!" He headed south and died in a mobile home park, alone and way too soon. Here is the saddest part of the story. I needed to reconcile the way I viewed our dad with the way he did. I had to know the truth and what had really happened. Delano would never hear the whole story, because he ran away.

My brother Bob Edwin did die of malnutrition. Delano had that part right. No one ever faced any punishment for his death nor was any vengeance paid. The question is who should pay for this crime? Who should answer for the death of a small innocent boy?

My dad was drafted into the military, in the latter part of WWII. He was sent to Europe, with his first wife and two sons were left in the US, alone.

As a pretext, I am not assigning blame. I am only stating what I learned. While dad was off in forced service, his first wife slipped into heavier drinking and spent time at the local watering hole. While she was out, my brothers were left alone.

Someone, source unknown, reported the situation Delano and Bob found themselves in. The result was both brothers were sent to the local social service for care. While in the care of the state, Bob Edwin passed away. My beautiful dark-haired brother starved to death as my oldest brother was forced to watch.

The person in charge of Bob's care was overburdened, thanks to the war in Europe. For years everything had been rationed, including supplies to the social services departments. My brothers and others at the home were given small portions. With an alcoholic mother, who had emotional issues, who was separated from her husband and was now separated from my brothers, tragedy was resting behind the door. The portions were small, but enough. My brothers and the others were left unattended after food was served.

So, to whom do we assign blame? Dad? Mom? The State? The overworked social worker? Hitler, for starting the war? Every aunt, uncle, cousin, friend, or neighbor who didn't step into the breach and save Bob Edwin? Or do we blame Delano for reaching across the table and taking a bite of Bob's food? Or do we blame the girl to his left or the boy to his right for doing the same. Or do we blame my beautiful dark-haired brother, who I only saw once in a photo, for not cowboying up and fighting for his right to eat?!

I cannot heal the scars for my brother, nor do I know to whom the vengeances are due. The list of suspects is too long, the details are too few, and my knowledge is too limited.

Why did God say, "vengeance is mine?" Because they are. He is the only one who knows the truth and can see the whole story.
Delano lost out on knowing the dad that I knew. He lost out on his relationships with his wives, children, and grandchildren, because he pulled at the thread of pain too long. The trick is to forgive when it hurts and let the scar heal. Believe that the sovereign of the universe will deal with the cause. Our job is to help as many people as we can, by helping them heal and rely on God. Matthew 6:14

I will see you both soon. Love Your Brother.

I Think of Pop *by Clay Octobre*

I think of Pop and a one on one.
Those special times when honesty was not undone.
As he held a coffee cup in his massive hands,
Our conversation was true, with no hidden strands.
Alone at the table, we would often chat.
Most of our talk was silly, light, and about this and that.
That morning however was not the same.
Pop spoke of his friend; Slim was his name.
Slim was a musician, a guitarist by trade.
At a very young age, some fame he had made.
As Pop spoke, he seemed to travel to a place.
The feelings were real and showed clear on his face.
He and Slim were going to town.
As Pop said it, to get their Honky-Tonk down.
His sadness was clear, by the tears in his eyes.
I set and I watch as the big man cries.
He told me what his best friend had done.
I was shocked as Pop spoke of hearing the gun.
The concussion, from the blast, filled the room.
Five decades after, Pop's face was filled with gloom.
He described what he found, as he continued to cry.
His best friend and cousin had chosen to die.
Pops' scar was clear in his face to see.
His pain and his heartbreak he shared with me.
He had no answers as to why.
He felt betrayed by Slim's lie.
It had been over fifty years since Slim passed away,
Yet Pop carried the burden to that day.
One thing I've learned and can now see,
Is the sadness he felt was passed on to me.
For twenty years later, while holding my cup,

My wife could see tears in my eyes as I stirred Pops' scar up.
I could see that I had passed it to her.
In time God will provide the cure.
But for now, we will simply have to be strong.
We must remember that God has had a plan all along.
If we must set and hold a big man's hand as tears fall,
Don't forget, heartache and sadness affect us all.
The Bible tells us at Revelation twenty-one verse four,
Jehovah God promises death and pain will be no more.
Until that day be courteous and kind.
Show your love and try not to leave any scars behind.
I love you Pop and I can't wait for the day
To hug your big neck, with our scars thrown away!

A Dose of Today *by Colleen Wells*

Take your medicine, the 150 mg of Buproprion
and 5 mg of Aripiprazole.
Take your Vitamin D.

Wash it down with cold water or orange juice.
Grab some coffee on the way out.

Grow your to-do list,
write it down in blue,
start on it.

Feel bored, get tired, wonder what it's all for.
You're wading in the muck now.
Let it pull you down into sleep.

Wake up at four-thirty.
Get back to doing.
Check the list again.

Only five things are checked off.
Make some coffee, take a walk.
The sun is out now.
This is as good as it gets
  for today.

The Serpent with Two Tales *by Colleen Wells*

Depression.
You will it away, but you're well-versed in sadness-
enough to know it doesn't work like that.

Go to bed early, wake up late.
It can't find you in your sleep
except for that one night
you dreamed of a serpent with two tails.

Try to remember what it felt like to laugh,
and realize the memory is like distant thunder.
Way. Way. In the distance.

When is the last time you danced in the kitchen,
or looked in the mirror and saw something pretty?
Where is the writer's high when time disappears
along with your cares?

Gone is the will to get excited over a call from a good friend,
the desire for anything specific to eat
except the coffee that keeps you going.

Drum up ways you could go,
pills and you can drift off to sleep,
except you might only take enough to damage
your brain, not shut it down.

Eye the door. Remember the scene in the movie
with the door and the belt.
But would what have worked for her, work for you too?
It was just a movie.

No option is optimal because you know deep down
you don't really want to die.
You just want it to stop.

Reframing *by Colleen Wells*

The bare limbs of the birch tree
jut out like skeleton arms,
and the bee balm
looks stringy and tired,
against a backdrop of sludgy snow.

The window framing my view
is dirty, and the plants along the ledge slouch
under winter's breath heaving in through the old panes of glass.

Maybe I should have gone to work after all,
or maybe I'm best at home.
Either way,
I've got to reframe my view.

My Amygdala *by D.A. Cairns*

Sometimes, when it's quiet, I can remember what my life was like before moving to Cedar Springs. When my thoughts had sharp edges, and my feelings were distinctly outlined by a shadow of self control. Before the colours began to blur, running together like water colours in rain. A time when I was in control, or at the very least, I confidently clung to the illusion of control as most of my fellow human beings do. Before moving to Cedar Springs, I was unhinging slowly, like a door which was being used as playground equipment. To say this move was important would be to grossly understate the fact. This move was life saving. This quiet and secluded house in Nowheresville had become my savior, and if my amygdala could have spoken, it would have cried with gratitude. Or would it?

The doctor had said it several times, as though I needed to know not only what it meant but how to pronounce it. A–myg-da-la. I was much more interested in what had gone wrong with it. I shook as I sat and listened: the lid on my anger barely restrained by the firm grip of my wife's hand on my arm. I had felt Alison's strength on previous occasions as it flowed from her hand through my body. It had been sufficient on all but two occasions. Now, as a direct result of the last of those occasions, she walked with a limp. And a proud scar bisected her left eyebrow as testimony to her bravery. I knew I should have run away from this woman who I had loved since the hormonal surge of adolescence propelled me towards manhood. If only for her sake, to protect her, but I was too afraid. Too scared to leave. Besides, I didn't know where to go. I often wished that when my lips devoured hers that I could have sucked courage from her like a baby suckles nourishment from its mother's breast.

The doctor had worn an expression of practiced sympathy as he sighed and spoke to Alison. I remembered his exact words.

'We don't properly understand what has caused this damage nor do we have any means to repair it.'

A sudden dramatic sadness collapsed on me when I saw a single tear roll down Alison's cheek. I had wanted to speak, to offer some solace but I was incapable: paralyzed by the darkest melancholy. The realization that I would not get better was disturbing. My impotence as a comforter to my wife was humiliating. So we both cried together inside a hopeless embrace.

Two months have passed, and I have not hurt Alison or myself. Somehow I have managed not to break anything. I feel relatively calm. As calm as I ever am, or can be. Lithonate apparently works well, to control the wild impulses associated with the manic phase of bi polar disorder, but I'm not bi polar. The doctor described my condition as something very much like bi polar disorder. He gave me a library of literature on bi polar and related mental illnesses, with a caveat that I was not bi polar and the research on the role of the amygdala was still in its early stages, so although I may find some of the information helpful, I should not count on it. I should not, he stressed, hang my hopes on it providing answers or solutions. I recall wanting to stuff all those brochures down his throat and watch him choke to death on them.

I have never read a single word because I cannot see how knowing what might be wrong with me, can assist me to carry on living with something less than the complete desperation that I feel most of the time. I take the pills that I have been prescribed and I attend a series of therapy sessions. I also try to make healthy life choices, which for me means that I don't start drinking until after lunch, and I torment myself on an elliptical cross trainer, albeit infrequently. I have very strong and emotionally intense memory flashes but I have learned how to manage them. The therapy sessions equipped me pretty well.

I feel depressed, and then elated, then depressed again before a callous attack of one phobia or another leads me back down into the hole of abject misery. I am exhausted so I sleep often, though never for more than a few hours. I live alone, and never leave the house in Cedar Springs. It is a fortress built to keep the protagonists in my private war in, rather than out. I am a menace, and I know it.

The telephone rings. Twice, then it stops. It rings again immediately, three times, then stops. When it sounds again, I pick it up and rest the receiver against my ear, breathing as quietly as I can though my heart is hammering in my chest, and I feel like I am suffocating.

'Bailey. It's me.'

'I know.'

'Then why don't you say anything when you pick up?'

I ignore Alison's question, partly because I figure she doesn't really want to know, but mostly because I don't know. She always contacts me using that agreed upon code, and every day I respond with the same inexplicable paranoia.

'What are you doing?'

'Sitting.'

'Just sitting?'

'Uh-huh.'

Words were dancing through my mind like fairies in an enchanted forest: words with no discernible intent. I can't speak. I'm glad she doesn't expect me to.

I feel hot and cold, feverish, as I listen to Alison talk about her day. She is trying to keep me connected but we both know that whatever binds a person to the society in which they live, has in my case, been terminally severed. I mumble and grunt in what I reason are appropriate places for such interjections. I am starting to experience heightened anxiety when I hear Alison say that she has to get back to work, but I don't know if it is because I am going to lose her again, or if some unspeakable evil is lurking at my door. There is always some hideous little beast waiting to pounce on me and tear me apart. That is what I fear now, as I say with as much sincerity as I can summon, 'I love you too. Bye.'

I hear laughter: the snickering of a mischievous child. Footsteps precede giggling. Stupid little girls hanging around outside the freak's windows trying to frighten themselves. Just having fun at my expense. Fun. Hilarity. I roar with amusement: a laugh so violently that I forget to breathe and am forced to the floor in a gagging fit. I laugh at myself. At the silly curious girls. At the absurdity of my imprisonment. And I laugh at my amygdala until my energy is totally depleted.

An alarm sounds but I don't recognize it at first. Initially, I confuse it with the sound of my voice which I notice has become shrill and hoarse. The alarm is a reminder to take another pill, and although I have not eaten lunch, it is after twelve so I can legally, according to my laws, wash the Lithonate down with a cold Carlton Draught. Great ads they make, I think. So funny. Funny? No, my laughter tank is dry. Clever. Who? Me or the beer ads? Pill? Yes please, and can I have fries with that? No, wait, on second thoughts, I'll take salad. After all, I'm supposed to be making healthy choices. Choices? Cigarettes. Do I smoke? I look at my watch and remember the Lithonate. I also notice that I have been standing still for half an hour. I feel a little better now.

I take my pill and swill my Carlton Draught in between puffs on a cigarette which surprisingly tastes stale. Maybe, I quit and forgot to throw these ones away. As I settle in my favourite chair in front of the television, my mind piggybacks my body into tranquility. My amygdala informs me, indirectly of course, that everything is alright for now. For now. This is my existence. I turn on the television and see straight edges and distinct shapes, and my hope is renewed.

Familiar voices soothe like Aloe Vera on sunburned skin. I know these people on the television, but they don't know me. I think my obscurity is an advantage but I can't explain why. No one would ever ask anyway because I don't have conversations. When the need arises - and thank God that is seldom - I approximate appropriate social intercourse. I can fake it with the best of them. They're all fakers. I know that too. It's comforting to be certain about some things in my life even though those things are so few in number, I can count them on one hand.

What do I know? Upon which facts can I suspend my existence? I'm alive. I live alone. I don't really belong anywhere or with anyone. Alison loves me. I'm grappling with the vagueness caused by ineffective synapses in my brain, searching for the fifth thing. Hoping like crazy that I can seize it and even, dare I dream, make it to my other hand and then I will have really achieved something today. I take a breath and glance over to the bookshelf stuffed with dust covered silverfish boarding houses. I can't read anymore. I just don't enjoy it. I'm busy lamenting my loss of literary interest when I hear Alison's voice. Although it's unmistakable, the most recognizable voice in my life, I hesitate as I try to figure out how I could be hearing her. I do hear voices. That's not unusual, but I've never heard of Alison. When I look at the television screen, I see her. She's doing an ad for a local pharmacy. Someone switches on a kettle in my stomach and I can feel the awful churning commence, the bubbling of emotions. I remember Alison studying for her degree, studying fervently, giving it everything she had. I recall criticizing her and calling her a dreamer.

High school drop outs don't go on to university, earn degrees and get high paying jobs, I said. She cried whenever I was mean to her, and she cried when I inevitably apologized, but I kept on hurting her. I didn't mean to. I've never intended to hurt anyone. I smile, but it's a pathetic one like the seven hundredth cheesy grin you've had to force for the endless photo shoot at a wedding. I'm glad Alison and I never married.

I was well when we met, perfectly well and we were perfectly happy. We crashed headlong into love from the first night we met at a mutual friend's birthday party. We talked and laughed. We flirted, we connected – there's an overused word – and I remember wishing that I could stay with her all night. Spellbound, I was trapped in her intoxicating energy. By the time I started having trouble with my amygdala, we were so deeply in love and committed to one another that we thought we could win. Foolishly, we believed that we were strong enough to overcome anything. The fairy tale ending would be ours. We deserved it. We were so wrong.

Looking at Alison, I see a princess. But she's not my princess. She's beautiful, kind, generous and intelligent. She's dogged as well though, and underneath her sweet and soft veneer, is a warrior. But she's not my warrior. I realize I'm crying when I can no longer clearly see her face. The ad ends with a happy jingle and an invitation to visit the store for the lowest prices and the best service. I want to go to her. I stand up but the room is spinning and I have to sit down. I won't be going to see her. I never leave my prison. I can't. Nothing is stopping me of course, except my own fear. I shudder and push my palms hard against my forehead. Can I reach my amygdala this way? Can I stop it? Can I crush this cruel dictator? I need some more pills. Did I miss the alarm? What time is it? Someone is yelling at me, telling me to get off my fat backside and do something useful. Be a man and stop wasting your life, it says. It sounds like my father but I never knew him. Or did I? I stand again, suddenly infused with anger. I want to hit something. Smash the source of that taunting voice. I feel hot as I listen carefully. Straining.

'It's only the size of an almond and you let it control your life,' says the voice.

I still can't tell from where these evil jibes emanate. I respond with, 'Actually it's not a single entity. It's a set of neurons located deep in the medial temporal lobe.' Where did that come from?

'Good for you. You know your enemy.'

'It's enlarged,' I continue. 'Damaged, so that it doesn't function properly. That's why I suffer all these mental problems.'

'Did you know that it shrinks by thirty percent in males after castration?'

'Who are you?'

I realize that I have walked into the kitchen during that conversation with an imaginary protagonist. A sense of déjà vu accompanies me. Maybe it's a good thing that my memory is faulty. When it works as it should, I have an overwhelming feeling that I have the same conversations every day, and do the same things. I don't know if this is true or not. It's not one of the five things I know for sure. That's right, the five things I know for sure. I recall trying to think of the fifth thing before I was distracted by the Warrior Princess on the television. Then it comes like a kingfisher dive bombing the surface of a creek for a feed: my amygdala is faulty, and it is to blame for my miserable existence. I am conscious of my shoulders sagging slowly under the weight of that depressing thought. I need a better one: a happy thought. I open the fridge. Everything is bright and fresh in there so I stand and stare, allowing the cold air to refresh me and renew my hope once more. Then it comes to me like benevolent lightning from heaven. Fact number six: I like beer. It's been a great day. I did something good and I can't wait to tell Alison all about it, if I can remember when she calls.

By Way of Explanation *by D.A. Cairns*

I have kept this journal going for nineteen years now but this will be my final entry. I briefly entertained the idea of giving this last installation of the serial of my life a fancy title like, By Way of Explanation: The circumstances surrounding, and the reasons for my suicide, but it sounded too pretentious and frankly, I couldn't be bothered. Never during the course of this written chronicle of the highs and lows of my life have I wasted words, so why begin now?

This journal of mine will be easily found, after my body is, because I will make no effort to conceal it. While I lived I would rather have died than allow anyone to read my intimate thoughts and deeds, but now on the eve of my death…well, I'm sure the irony does not escape you.

No doubt the person who finds me, and my journal, will go straight to the last entry in a search of answers. So it is answers I will attempt to provide. Whether they will prove satisfactory to whomever reads or hears them, I cannot know. I will be dead, and despite the adult fairy tale about our loved ones looking down from heaven which we use to comfort ourselves, I will be gone and no longer interested in or in touch with this world. Dead is dead, I reckon. When I leave this thing called time, I'll be somewhere else-that's assuming there is any existence after death-out of time.

Apart from fantastic Hollywood images of Heaven and Hell, and a knowledge instilled in me during my childhood about the rules for who goes where, I really have no idea what awaits me on the other side.

I'll tell you one thing though, I am not afraid. I fear neither the process of death nor the uncertainty of what lies beyond the act itself. I have given it a lot of thought, maybe too much thought. That, I think, has been one of my more serious problems, too much thinking.

53

No matter how I have reasoned it out, I cannot convince myself that death is something to be avoided. I have never feared death, and now I have or should I say, now I will, prove it.

To the inevitable question which arises; why? Why did I kill myself? It strikes me as amusing to talk of myself in the past tense so I will continue that way. Why did I kill myself? People say things like, he hated himself, he hated life, he was depressed, unhappy, lonely, he couldn't find a reason to live. All reasonable points and possibly true in many instances but not at all applicable to me.

My life was not marked by undue suffering. My upbringing was normal. Mum loved me, so did Dad in his own way. He was away from home often on business trips and was consequently a distant father in both senses of the word, but he provided well for his family. Nothing went wrong. I had no disabilities or tragedies with which to contend.

Admittedly, I was very shy and this caused me to come to prefer my own company, and therefore be perceived as a loner. However, I had a few good friends whom I trusted and liked, so I wasn't lonely. I had a secure, well paying job with an international financial institution, and married an impossibly sweet and beautiful woman with whom I had two bright and healthy children.

It all sounds great doesn't it? So far, all I've done is give good reason to live, not to die. No grounds in any of that for dissatisfaction with the world. No cause for complaint about life and how she treated me. What then was my problem?

I remember one day, a zealous young Christian approached me on the street, his face alight with joy and bannered with a wide smile. After introducing himself he told me how Jesus had posed the question, what does it profit a man to gain the whole world yet forfeit his own soul? I told him to get fucked.

I always felt there was something missing in my life, something not quite right. Although I could not identify it exactly, I knew there was something wrong with my life and by logical extension, something wrong with me. When I say always, I really mean particularly from about the age of fifteen. More specifically, the first time I got drunk on a bottle of cheap wine in the grounds of my old school. I remember well the delicious euphoria of intoxication and the thrill of doing something so 'naughty', and how quickly that glorious feeling disappeared when I unloaded the contents of my stomach on the grass a few hours later.

If I need to apologize for all this wandering down memory lane, then I do. I recognize how self indulgent it is, but it's my journal and just in case you weren't able to work it out while I was with you, this is who I am.

Any suggestion that I ended my life because I hated myself is wrong. The truth is, I loved myself too much to allow me to suffer that existence any longer. It should be called a mercy killing, not a suicide.

If there was one event which pushed me over the edge and helped me to finally decide upon this course of action, then it was the disintegration of my marriage. My wife left me, and although we were both at fault for the break-up, I didn't love her enough to accept my share of the blame. I didn't love her enough to say I was wrong and to ask her forgiveness. I was the only victim and damn it all if I would not hold onto that pain.

I know I pushed her away from me and into the strong embrace of a better man than me but it was her choice to be unfaithful. Wronged, I loved myself too much to forgive her even though I too was guilty of breaking our marital vows.

No, I didn't have an affair, but I gutlessly abrogated my responsibilities as a husband and a father. I was unfaithful to her and after a while I stopped trying or even pretending to care.

The separation and subsequent divorce caused me more suffering than I showed to anyone so I tried to comfort myself by saying that I deserved to be treated better than that. It doesn't matter anymore, anyway. My marriage is history and so am I. Me, the man who loved his children and his wife and everyone else in his life, only when they pleased him. No person could please me all the time and I just grew tired of expecting so much from people, and being continually let down. No hate though, I never hated. Not even toward my job did I bear any ill feeling. It simply bored me.

Lack of stimulation in my life caused me no end of frustration. I dreamed of much yet achieved nothing and my failures were always someone else's fault. I couldn't stand it anymore.

To all my friends and family who loved me despite my selfishness, I want to say thank you for trying to make my life bearable. Some of you may also be hoping for an apology from me, expressing my sorrow for the pain I have caused you, but I think rather that I should be congratulated for relieving you of the burden of having to tolerate me. If I'm sorry, it is only in this, that you may fail to be grateful for the favor I have done you.

My final request, if I may be so bold, is that you not sentimentalize my life as I've always felt disappointed by the lack of honesty at funerals. The bottom line is that I'm gone, I'm dead, and some of you are glad about that which is okay because I'm glad I'm dead too.

***

If you or anyone you know is contemplating suicide, please call 988. The 988 Suicide & Crisis Lifeline is a national network of local crisis centers that provides free and confidential emotional support to people in suicidal crisis or emotional distress 24 hours a day, 7 days a week, in the United States. See the Resources section for more information.

Light Patterns are My Delight *by Diana Humphrey*

They change as I watch or as I move.
They wait for me at every time of day
and in every place. You could say
I was blessed. With them I am never alone.

My eye and brain constantly engage
because of them. They cannot be ignored,
though of course, they are silent.
Sometimes, because of them,

I move soundlessly in my house.
At night, when the moon is strong,
I pad downstairs to find them spread
over the table, poured over the tiled floor.

The sky through the glass roof
lives in my space now. In sunlight
or firelight the stained glass transom
over the door casts stains, the angled

glass vase shoots shards of white light
on the pale wood. The curve of the arch
shifts its shadows down the chrome
lampstand. I polish mirrors and brasses

solely for their reflections
and refractions. Hundreds jostle
always for my attention.
Light patterns are my delight.

The Pair of Curtains *by Diana Humphrey*

Anne-Marie couldn't remember where she'd got the lounge curtains from but she could put a good spin on anything. She was 'a born storyteller' her nanny used to say with that funny look on her face. So she would offer the version that sprang to her mind that minute. She'd swapped them with a rag-and-bone man for a £50 note. They'd been in the attic. They were a gift, an inheritance.

Everyone remarked on them. The curtains in question were magnificent, sumptuous and even here looked out of place. They belonged somewhere even grander.

'My God', one of her husband's cousins had once said, 'Where did you steal those from? The Chinese Room at Versailles?' Sheila was always name dropping to make sure you knew how well travelled she was. Anne-Marie and Robin told people they were now home birds. 'East, West, Home' best they'd chant together and hug each other. People were charmed.

They didn't know about Anne-Marie's agoraphobia since she'd lost the baby. It was fixed in her head that if she had not wanted one last visit to Madeira before the baby was born, one last walk in the high hills along the water channels, the lavadas they were called, they'd have a family of their own now. In her head she knew that, if anything, it was the guide's fault. He should have chosen the route with more care after that heavy rainfall and maybe then she wouldn't have slipped and all would have been well.

'You can't change the past!' They all told her that and, 'Second time lucky!' but Anne-Marie was too sunk in grief and guilt to be able to think ahead and too paralyzed by guilt and grief to have the will to leave her home. Together she and Robin managed well enough preserving the appearance of normality and keeping the house going though it was difficult.

Tim, their gardener, cared for the outside and each time he visited made a video as requested. Anne-Marie had told him she was keeping a journal of the year's progress. In actuality she was sending out her regular blog on her imaginary lifestyle and her all-consuming garden under the pen name of Daisy's Dream. She had a large and loyal following.

The couple ordered everything they needed on line and had stuff delivered including new frocks for Anne-Marie to wear when she acted as hostess in their own house. Manicurists, hairdressers, exercise therapists called regularly. Robin went to work as usual and kept up with their social set and brought home all the gossip. Anne-Marie spent hours on the phone ringing friends and contacts, the hours when she wasn't prowling round the empty house weeping. The nursery door stayed shut though every detail of its pale blue and yellow décor, its cupboard full of baby clothes, its shelves of books and soft toys, were inscribed on Anne-Marie's heart.

Sometimes she wanted to run away, anywhere. She once even got as far as the porch in her coat, bag and keys in her hand, before crumpling on the floor, shaking and sobbing with tension. When Robin came home, though, he'd always find her composed and professional, a meal ready to eat after what they called their cocktail hour. He saw the pain in her eyes, saw how she was losing weight but did not know what to do to help her. He hoped that this was a necessary stage in the mourning of the lost baby and all would be well before long. Till then he thought it best to play the game.

If you could have watched them through the French windows, smiling at each other, raising toasts in the Chablis, nibbling the exotic dishes she had heated from the freezer all beautifully served on pretty dishes by candlelight you might have envied them. But theirs is a story with a heart of darkness and a dilemma to solve. Anne-Marie, as you know, is deep in misery, ashamed of her weakness and seeing no future for herself and Robin. She must be saved, she is worth it. She has courage, she loves life, she loves her husband. So what can help her?

As you know, too, in a story wonderful things can happen and one day they did. Anne-Marie was standing at her wide windows, looking out at the garden, watching the breeze toy with the tops of the red-hot-pokers and bend the bamboo and elephant grass in the distant border. Her hand was gently stroking the edge of one of her magnificent curtains, over and over again. She could not know this but she was exactly reflecting the extraordinary moment Ali Baba rubbed the magic lamp. Her fingers were moving across one of the pagodas stitched in silver on the heavy Oriental brocade. Over and over they moved. She had never caressed the cloth like this before. It engrossed her and more wonderfully, calmed her.

Finally she let her right hand drop from the cloth and her left undo the latch of the French window. Of their own accord her feet stepped onto the patio and directed her over the lawn to stand under the cedar tree. She had never been so far and never felt so at peace. She gazed up into the dark branches and tears of joy streamed down her face.

She knew she had changed, been freed, and was ready to start living again. She was still outside wandering happily round all the plants that gardener, Tim, had videoed for her over so long while she was held captive inside, when Robin came out looking anxious. He called her name. She turned and when he saw her wide smile and the light in her eyes he smiled too and held out his arms to hold her.
Of course, we know anxieties and phobias are seldom dispatched with magic but this is a story, so just this once, why don't we have an ending which is unequivocally happy?

Hidden Demons *by EB Hills*

I reached out to grasp my demons
but they are not there.
I've seen them on television,
imagined the pain, violence, fear, agony:
bloody hands, torn away limbs,
graves in sand pits watered by tears
of wives, children, parents.

I know that deep pain
yet can't feel it.
It's there in my nightly dreams,
an immense dark figure
hovering, pressing,
draining my small life.

I turn palms up
and trace thin white lines
from wrist to elbow.
You nod and encourage,
give me the space to seek,
to step into the darkened abyss,
help me believe there will be
a net to catch my fall.

Thankless *by EB Hills*

Long is the journey
from warm womb to stony grave
for the thankless one

Pay It Forward *by EB Hills*

Don't wait for tragedy
to pry open a
kindness in your demeanor,
tug at your heart, your brain,
clear your vision to the pain,
sorry, destitution of others.
Look now, really look
into their eyes, smile
and offer something
other than a spare coin -
a hand, shoulder,
piece of your heart.
Ask nothing in return,
and let it pay forward.

Bridges from Battle Scars *by Elizabeth Cox*

I have had many dark times in my life and many days of good.
I would not change one single thing, even if I could.

Our lives are like the ocean, sometimes stormy, sometimes calm.
Most days we step confidently into that ocean, other days we have
qualms.

The waves, ebb and flow, are sometimes trials from our Father.
God helps us build a bridge of battle scars to cross these troubled
waters.

The harder times are allowed and good times given from above.
The blessing that I was given is to know God's unconditional love.

The one thing we need to remember is that we never walk alone.
God is there right there beside us until the day He leads us home.

Heavenly Healing *by Elizabeth Cox*

From the time we are born, we all have accidents. We fall or make bad choices, and we hurt ourselves. Oftentimes someone else hurts us. Sometimes it's just a bruise or a small insignificant injury, but other times it's traumatic, and you have to have stitches or surgery, or the injury is so great that a scar is left behind, which reminds you of what happened and the pain it caused you.

We are not always hurt physically. Sometimes it is emotional pain or a combination of the two. People are often cruel with their words and actions and hurt us with something they say or do. It hurts our feelings, and the damage caused leaves an intangible cut or tear in our heart, which eventually will heal on its own over time.

Then there are the traumatic injuries, such as when a loved one dies or your spouse divorces you, the times where the pain or grief is so severe that it affects us physically. These are the events that cause the big cracks in our heart. Unseen by human eyes, but God knows.

God sees the cracks. God sees the tears. He knows that without His intervention, we will not be able to handle the pain. He holds us in His arms and comforts us along the way as He heals our heart and, layer by layer, builds a scar to cover that crack so we don't feel the pain, or at least it's not so devastatingly intense.

Eventually, although it can sometimes take a lifetime, we don't feel the pain from what caused the scar unless thoughts lead us back due to a memory of a smell, a touch, or something we see. I truly believe that God loves us so much that He does not want us to be in pain. He knows that unless he covers that injury with a scar it will always bring us pain. So the scar is lovingly created a layer at a time until it is complete. Thank you, Heavenly Father, for our scars.

Out of My Mind *by Isabella St. Kim*

I fell in love and lost my mind

I listened to his voice instead of mine

His lifestyle, his habits, his friends somehow became mine

What was I thinking

I was out of my mind

The way he listened and responded to my needs

I fell for it all with such great ease

I must have been out of my mind

Time moved on and I noticed one change

My feelings for you are not the same

I must have been out of my mind to let things go on just the same

I finally opened my eyes towards you

I finally found real peace of mind without you

And now, I'm no longer out of my mind

Tears of Grief by Isabella St. Kim

Tears of grief aren't confined by time and place

They never announce their schedule or duration of stay

Happy one moment, teary eyes the next

Please don't impose your feelings of when and how I should react

Allow my mind and body to process my loss

Let me do what I need to do to reestablish my thoughts

Let me cry without any guilt

When did mourning have a designated start and end point

My life has changed; readjusting to new things

My memories are the tears that you see

For now, let me be me

White Demons *by Isabella St. Kim*

Shades of black may resemble white

With the swiftness of evil they can turn white

Friendly one moment, deadly the next

Meanwhile, mastering their talents while under disguise

They call themselves your "friend" yet will lead you astray

Before you know it, you've become their prey

Their ability to lead you into darkness, while fading when exposed to light

They are only waiting for you to backslide, then they will strike

Black demons hide no secrets

White demons are subtle, making them dangerous to detect and react

Golden Eagles *by Jason Bayliss*

Life ahead truly does lie sharp, radiant and bold.

And sharp and pointy with jagged edges, sometimes.

And sometimes so full of warmth and light that you forget all hurts and sorrows, if only for a moment.

And the light is bright enough to see the scars that make your story, and warm enough to heal them.

And the past is your guide and template for the future, and in that you'll find comfort and pain, but mostly comfort.

Yours is a beautiful light my friend and like all light it shines brightest in the darkest hours.

The hours when the meek hide beneath the covers and the bold light up the world.

Never let that light diminish, it is too beautiful, too radiant to be veiled in darkness.

All that eagles need to soar is an open sky and a brave heart. You have both, stretch those wings.

Walk The Paths Well Trodden By The Brave
by Jason Bayliss

Walk the paths well trodden by the brave,
Live boldly my son, embrace your fears and let them drive you on,
Be master of your hurts not slave,
Value the story in your scars, pity those that have none.
Treasure every tear that rolls on your cheek,
Let them fall on barren ground knowing their waters bring life,
Their salt does not cleanse the lips of the meek,
In the same way as those that shoulder their strife.
Let your heart be broken a dozen times,
Rather than close it in fear of all that would break it,
In love be fierce but never blind,
Love true and honest so that none can mistake it.
Face your end with a defiant smile,
Recount all the steps that have led you hence,
Insist that the reaper tarry a while,
Enjoy a few moments at his expense.
And in that final time, when he asks,
Fix him with a gaze both firm and steady,
Acknowledge that he has, "Other tasks," And calmly say, "I'm ready."

Ripped at the Seams *by Jessica Oakwood*

When psychosis broke me apart
delusions and confusion.
I struggled to make sense of all the pieces
of my identity that had shattered.
Some pieces could be
stuck back together with figurative
masking tape. But others had splintered off
unrepairable. And so I set to
fix these cracks, fractures, broken pieces
using the Japanese art of kintsugi.
Using gold joinery, precious self awareness,
to piece myself back to together
like a broken bowl.
do it yourself identity.
DIY spirituality,
on a deeper level than the golden seams.
They say that
people always keep their eyes on the places
where the cracks are,
but for me,
I accepted these breaks
as part of me
in the grander scheme of my history.
Now I worry less that I am broken
instead I have really lived
although it is a life that I wouldn't choose
who wants to be a schizophrenic, or schizoaffective,
whatever luggage tag they use
for my baggage.

Instead, I am whole again
with these experiences
holding me together
stronger.

Take Me Home *by John Ganshaw*

Forever lost and can't be found
fan spinning above your head
winds of strength keep the demons away
they still see the hurt and pain
try to lure the soul to the other side
long to live but some must die
the heart burns and the memories stay
all that lingers in the mind
always moving nowhere to hide
think about all that was
happiness and smiles for those to see
inside of you, the whole world bleeds
tears of joy don't exist
hope is lost in a distant place
caricatures of who we are
evil lurks all around
seeks you out in the dead of night
haunts you with a lullaby
kicking, screaming you fight to wake
shaking, crying all alone
begging to be taken home
life isn't always grand
saving those when others won't
tear you down at every chance
no time to hate but yet despise
pay the price for others' crimes
how it ends no one knows
choices to be made
fade to darkness the sun has gone
he is hiding in the shadows
watching and waiting

time goes by and who will win
will to live or will to leave
breathe the air, stay alive
let it go don't hold on
every day there is a dawn
the future is bright they say
the path is hidden by the trees
close your eyes
live your life as meant to be
kiss their lips then move on
wash away what was done
the past was then and now you're here
today will soon be yesterday
tomorrow will always come
sorrow and sadness seem to thrive
these thoughts are not meant to be
each day just try to stay alive

Please Don't Go *by John Ganshaw*

In the darkest days, when all is lost
The despair is there in every breath
The struggle to go on, overwhelming
You want it all to end
Seeking a better place to open your eyes

You sit and wonder, gazing hopelessly
You ask yourself how do I get there?
Can I take a plane?
Can I take a train?
Perhaps a bus will leave me there

There are no paths to lead you
You can't walk
There are no lights to guide you
There are no streams to follow
Only through the utter darkness can you get there

Through pills, you can make an attempt
Perhaps a knife is the ticket
A gun, and a rope, are options for this trip
But will you awaken
No guarantee you will open your eyes

We do not know where all will lead
If we did wouldn't everyone want to go
I think it's best to stay and dream
Dream of the place where all is good
This is where we can open our eyes
This is where we will survive

To stay where we can breathe
A place we know and can exist
We are meant to stay in the light
We can't succumb to the dark
This is hard, this I know
We are the strong to continue this fight
Why should we go
The best place is here

Escape From the Shadows *by John Ganshaw*

It took so long to find the light, and see the brightness that exists
Years went by when only shadows were known; the darkness felt
All those years of breathing and not living, scared and lonely
Afraid to feel the warmth of another, believing how you felt
Wasn't right, normal to love and care for another man
Tense when you felt the embrace, a soul longing for love but
Uncomfortable within the skin that was its home
A heart full of warmth for others yet cold to itself
Years of believing it was all a dream, an escape from reality
Was what you sought. Fifty years of escape before the truth
Was revealed to you. From the shadows of the past you saw
That little boy steps out, a grown man now but no longer hidden
And ashamed of what happened. Realizing it wasn't your fault, he
Molested you, he shamed you and made you believe. Years of
Abuse that followed and haunted your presence. Always wanting
To please yet never you. Lived for others but never you. Protecting
Others but never you. Saving others but never you. Now you see
All the past, Now you can fight all those battles within. You know
The truth and no longer in shame, you moved on and now you
Bear witness that the little boy in the mirror is finally free.

Eroded *by Julie A. Dickson*

If I never go down this path again
I may return to what I was.
Circuitous path through brambled
oak, gnarled places where branches
once grew, cut or broken off, no time
to heal, just sealed memories entwined
in places I thought would be mine,
if not for what came before, up against
a wall, closed door against thought,
times I forgot, pain faded to dull, recall
only the good – fool I was, not knowing
hiding beneath the hood, blind eye turned,
I learned to embrace the now, for what
I can hold in my hand, like wispy strands
of hair flowing through a brush, eroded sand,
divot in my heart filling with tidewater.

Running Red *by Julie A. Dickson*

Stark white handkerchief he handed to her
                suggested surrender
to wipe at the corner of bloodied lips
                as if by accident
this had occurred rather than by hand
                raised and struck
She peered down at this crimson smear
                would never wash
out, not from white cotton, nor memory
                permanent stain
slashed like the knife held to white skin
                trickle of blood
mesmerized, hypnotized her face blank
                but for single tear
rolling silently down plump brown cheek
                wrists running red

Scary Mara *by Julie A. Dickson*

Why am I feeling this way? Mara Willard wondered as she smoothed the crumpled skirt she wore to school. She pulled a small mirror from her purse, sneaking a quick glance at herself before Mr. Hughes caught her. She felt like screaming, but Mara took a deep breath, hoping that the anxiety she was feeling would go away.

"She's insane," Mara heard the whisper from the girl behind her and to the left, heard a small snicker from Susan, who sat right behind her. Mara sunk down into her chair and tears burned her eyes.

Mr. Hughes rambled on as he wrote on the whiteboard in the front of the classroom. At least he hadn't noticed them making fun of her. She hated when he drew attention to her in class.

Mara reached into her pocket and felt the pill that she longed to take right now. She glanced up at the wall clock; 11:25 am, only five more minutes. Her hand squeezed against the pill, willing the time to move forward on the clock. 11:26. Mara could visualize herself walking quickly from the room, the reason why her preferred seat was in the closest row to the door. When the bell rang, her plan was to make a dash for the door; the water bubbler was only a few feet down the hallway. The pill would be on her tongue by the time she breached the doorway; the cool water inviting Mara in her mind. 11:27.

The anti-anxiety pill was the necessary crutch that Mara leaned on at school to get her through the day. Her shrink, ok therapist [right, mom…] appointment was later in the afternoon; but Mara was sick of Dr. Bloom trying to convince her that her problems were going away! 11:30 and there was the bell!

Dr. Bloom closed her eyes while Mara reclined in the huge, moss green chair in the corner of her office. Mara was one of her more challenging patients. No matter what methods Dr. Bloomed tried with Mara; hypnosis, medication therapy, meditation, positive reinforcement, the sixteen year-old showed no improvement. She looked over at Mara, who fidgeted in the chair, her hands moving across her clothing, her ankle bouncing over the edge of the foot rest. "Mara, take a deep breath and relax."

The doctor knew Mara's mother; she saw her weekly, in the attempt to decipher their family dynamics. An only child, this girl was under plenty of pressure to succeed. She had only met Mara's father Dan once, but Kimberly Bloom was pretty well convinced that the mother, Rose Willard, was much more influential with her daughter. Mara looked no more relaxed after her 3 moments of silence. Dr. Bloom insisted that they start each session with this quiet period of breathing and quiet; she hoped it would help Mara to focus.

"Ok, Mara. I want you to close your eyes and think about something nice from when you were young." She paused for a moment. "Now, tell me what you are thinking about."

Mara opened her lips to speak, "I'm at Gram's house. We're baking banana bread; I loved her banana bread." Mara smiled, her eyes still closed.

Dr. Bloom had planted the something nice suggestion in hypnosis, and now when she spoke the phrase to Mara, she immediately launched into little anecdotes, which were predominantly about her grandmother. "What else do you see? Is your mother there with you?"

Mara squirmed and looked uncomfortable in the chair, "We finished baking and mom picked me up. I don't want to go, Gram!" Dr. Bloom made some notes.

"Would you like a glass of water, Mara?" Dr. Bloom asked, breaking Mara's concentration, the phrase to bring Mara back. The girl nodded. The doctor nodded imperceptibly as she walked to the side of the room to pour Mara's water; it's not the grandmother. Mara was happy with her grandmother. It was obvious that they were close; it was clearly the mention of Mara's mother that caused her strong reaction!

Mara accepted the glass and managed a weak smile. Kimberly realized that she needed to do a lot more investigation with Rose Willard.

"Am I crazy?" Mara asked, biting her lip.

"No; you are not crazy." Dr. Bloom said firmly.

Mara waved her hand in the air, "Fine then, insane".

"Not insane. You don't show signs of insanity. I know that you feel anxiety, but that is not the same thing. Mara; don't you worry". Dr. Bloom laid one warm hand briefly on her patient's shoulder.

Hopeless Wish *by Karuna Mistry*

I cannot give you anything more
Cannot hug or see your face
I miss you for all of my days
Why did you have to leave?

If only you could have stayed
Another year, a week or day
Even that would not be enough
I would keep you forever

Many things I never told you
A few things I never showed you
Questions I don't know the answer to
Many more things we could do

Certain memories etched in me
While others will fade to grey
"Don't worry about me," you said
You must have known your fate

But I will always cherish
The very last thing
You ever spoke:
"Thank you…"

Stop *by Karuna Mistry*

I stopped
I stopped my life
I stopped my life for yourself
~
Put everything on hold
My wife, my child
My music, my home
My projects, my hobbies
My trips and travels
~
Even my work life
Interrupted sleep
Woken at night
Run myself down
If I don't stop.

You stopped
You stopped my life
You stopped my life for yourself
~
In your time of need
For months on end
I would do it all again
To serve you, cook for you
And be by your side
~
You did the same for me
In my younger days
It is no question then
Hear no complaint from me
Until you stop.

Because of You *by Karuna Mistry*

Because of you
I found myself
   How creativity lay dormant
   Stuck upon that bookshelf

Because of you
I renewed myself
   Turned over a new page
   Learnt how writing soothes oneself

Because of you
I am at the doorstep
   Found a new day job
   My career calls the next step

Because of you
I have a new interest
   Perform for creativity
   My gut I now trust

All because you lay
Lay in my arms that day
   Because of you
   Because of your death

Soul Scars *by Kathy Chaffin Gerstorff*

There you are beaming at everyone you meet,
posting highlights, keeping it together.

But, I see your soul scars.

Loneliness, heartbreak, addiction, apathy,
disappointment, depression, despair...

It's enough to turn most souls to dust,
but not us.

Diamonds are made from coal under pressure.
Show your scars and shine on!

Kintsugi *by Kathy Chaffin Gerstorff*

Precious china, shattered,
after the fall.

No longer valued,
or wanted at all.

Enter the ancient mending art of
Kintsugi,
where broken pieces
are filled with gold.

How befitting.
God did the same thing for me.

Filled my shattered heart
with His love, mended me.
Kintsugi.

It's stronger now.

Withstands rejection,
love grown cold,
a life full of toxic mold.

Despite it all,
my heart beats bold,
with the patches of gold.

What a sight to behold.

Petrichor *by Kathy Chaffin Gerstorff*

Instead of inhaling

doom and gloom,

let's take a walk

in the woods,

play hide and seek

among willow trees,

feel the sun rejuvenate our souls,

become one with dirt and rain,

bath in the healing fluid from mother nature's veins,

petrichor,

just what the doctor ordered.

Shadow Dancing *by Kathy Chaffin Gerstorff*

In the shadow of sleeping Kings,
soldiers, and poets,
comes another battlefield day.

Man against man, invisible wars,
hell's fury unleashed among trees.

Yet, upon the rocky shore,
angels dance and sing,
reminding us there is something more
than misery.

Light seeps into broken things.
Hope is on the horizon.

So on the solemn days,
let's find something to be grateful for,
like the sun upon our face,
and soothing soul songs.

Life Review *by Kathy Chaffin Gerstorff*

Will my life review show that I tried
despite repeated failures,
paralyzing insecurities,
and scar tissue in my heart?
Will I see a wasted life,
one of mediocrity,
of sadness masked by a smile?

Or will I see my life was as it should be
abundance all around me.

Will I feel when the sun warmed me
clear through to my soul?

Will I remember being one with nature,
grateful to be alive?

Will I see my smile reflected
in the eyes of a child?

Will I know my words
inspired someone?

My life review doesn't have to be at the end of my life.
It can be at the end of my day.

Did I show kindness,
compassion,
love?

Am I grateful for this one precious life
I get to experience another day?

I pray my daily life review
guides me
to the light within,

and helps others
find their way
out of the darkness.

Healing Hearts *by Kathy Chaffin Gerstorff*

My soul knows your soul.
My scars match your scars.
We misunderstood our connection.
It was not meant to be of the flesh or ego.
It was divine intervention,
guiding us to our Earthly assignment.
A calling to use our trauma to learn the power of forgiveness
and unconditional love.
Then share a message of hope from our healing hearts
to the world, at this appointed time, so all will know we are one.
Your pain is my pain.
Your joy is my joy.

Scar Salve *by Kathy Chaffin Gerstorff*

Take care not to stare at your scars
so long they consume you.

Rise above the pain of your past.

Let the salve of forgiveness heal you,
set your spirit free.

You do it for you.
I'll do it for me.

Together we will turn our wounds into a testimony
and go on a healing spree!

A Gift to a Gentile Lady *by Leland P. Gamson*

"Don't bury your dog Liddy's remains in the backyard."
Ruth was warned by her mother,
"Because if you do, whenever you see her grave, you will feel sad."
But Ruth did bury Liddy in their backyard
Not wanting her pals remains cremated then forgotten.
And Ruth buried other treasurers
Where she would keep running into them.

On her library shelf
She buried her high school yearbook
With photos of boys
Who didn't requite her crushes.
In her closet
She buried her ballet slippers
She can still fit into.

She buried in her trunk
Rejection letters from two
Seven Sister colleges
With letters from her boyfriend
Who wouldn't marry her
After she became pregnant.
And she buried on the shelf
A book of possible names
For their baby
She aborted.

Now thirty years later
She listens to the King of the Jews saying,
"My precious child take ballet lessons again.
Attend your high school reunion and meet
A redeemed brother I have prepared

To be your Boaz.
And if you can see through the glass darkly
You will see
In my Father's Kingdom
Your now named child
Plays with Liddy."

Guardian Bear *by Leland P. Gamson*

I, guardian bear, sit by the grave
Of a child whose stay here was brief
His day of birth, was not one of joy
Instead, it brought sorrow and grief

But were I, more than a stuffed bear
I 'd show you the Kingdom above
You'd see that our child is under God's care
Embraced by His angels and love.

The Power of My Daddy's Words *by Lori Jo Goss-Reaves*

My dad, Larry Jo Goss was killed in action in Vietnam on Valentines Day 1968 in the Quang Tri Province of Vietnam. Living without him was the hardest thing I've ever done. I used to study fathers and daughters. Peering from the outside onto those relationships made me miss my dad even more. Daddies play a vital role in the lives of their little girls. My dad would have played his role of daddy very well. He had the opportunity to do so for six months and in that short time he left me words that are sustaining me fifty-five years after his death. I praise God for my Daddy's words.

When I was in the fourth grade my teacher gave us an assignment to write about our wish. I wrote this essay, and my mom saved it. I thank God that she did.

My Wish

My dad got killed in the war. I was six months old. Mom didn't get back the dog tags. He may have been captured because he was a doctor. I have just about stopped wishing that he was just captured and come back. My grandma still believes he's alive.

We have his diary, pictures, slides, and tape recordings in a lockbox. I will go through it someday. It doesn't bother me to talk about him, it's the letters that upset me.

If he came back, it would help all our family. Especially Mom. They were only married for a year. My grandma has cancer and he's about the only thing she has to live for.

I don't know what it's like to have a real father. So, if I had one wish that would come true it would be that dad was just captured and would come back soon.

Jo (my teacher's name for me that entire school year)

My grandma died the following year, but my wish continued. My fear continued too. The fear was that my mom would die, and my half-brother and I would be orphans. I prayed to God that my mom would not die. She was not sick, but death was too much a part of my reality. I was a little girl but my awareness of the harsh reality of death surpassed many adults.

When I was fourteen, I wrote my first poem about my dad. My mom wanted to make sure he was not forgotten. She asked me to write something to put in the newspaper as a memorial. I prayed and these words easily flowed:

My Dad

Dad died fourteen years ago today,
What he was like I can't really say.

I was only six months old,
But many great things about him I have been told.

He had a lot of love deep within his heart,
But it was God's will that he and the world should part.

I used to lie in bed at night and think of him and cry,
Then the Lord made me realize it was for the best so I should hold my head up high.

And be proud of my father for giving this country his all,
Then giving his life when the Lord came to call.

To tell my dad "I love you" was a chance I never had
So I wrote this poem to dedicate it to Larry Jo Goss, my dad.

Lori Jo Goss
February 14, 1982

My understanding of God grew over the years but my yearning for my dad never waned. Though loss was always a part of my life I learned to focus on the present. Genetics helped me tremendously. Both of my parents had a cheerful disposition and a positive outlook on life. My parents also had a great sense of humor. Although I was more serious, their positivity was a part of my DNA. For this I am extremely thankful. Life is hard, hope is vital, and love makes it all worthwhile.

My dad's love for my mom and me was undeniable. He left evidence of it in every letter and audio tape he mailed home from Vietnam. His voice was cheerful. He was living under the stress of war every day yet his concern for us and our well-being was paramount. He ended each diary entry with the words "God bless Marty and Lori. God bless my family." He ended his letters telling my mom to "Sleep Warm" and "Kiss Lori For Me." He knew he might not make it home from the war alive. He wanted us to be happy, safe, and loved. He died for our freedom. I thank God for my mom and dad's love. One day I will get that kiss from him in heaven, and my mom will sleep warm beside him once again.

Lori Jo Goss-Reaves
Author of *Kiss Lori For Me*
Patagonia Press
Published July 20, 2022

Life is Better *by Marcia Durant*

You know what? My life is so much better....
There are no disagreements or major distractions or major decisions to be made. I cannot really believe how much quieter things are in two years. It took some time and finally things are calm. I can do what's best for me. I can set my boundaries. I can travel on the weekends and on vacation times and holidays. I don't have to run it by anyone else. I didn't realize all the years I was walking on eggshells. How much anxiety I had every time I heard the front door open and slam shut. There was a dark shadow hanging over my head. It took me a while to see the difference. Unhappiness comes from the negativity of others, the condemnation, the years of the belittling of your thoughts and opinions and 9 times out of 10 being told you are wrong about most everything you thought you were right about. Not every single thing but 95%. The only stress and drama now are from the things that break and trying to figure out how to fix them. I'm learning to deal with those things and learning to ask for help where needed. My beliefs are my own now and NOT those of someone else. IF I want to help my children I can and I'm not chastised for that. I have not been yelled at for 2 years and I'm not afraid of making mistakes because they happen. The Word is FREEDOM, "My chains are gone I've been set free." For those of you in new relationships pay attention, to your happiness, to your children's happiness, be aware of how you are treated. Don't commit to long term unhappiness, don't be afraid to be your own person, express your own thoughts and don't let them undermine what you know and feel is right. Be happy!! Don't settle for less.

Life of Depression *by Marcia Durant*

Is there more than this?
My life is just a dark abyss
I want to stay inside for now
Visitors I will not allow
To myself I'd rather stay
It's so much easier this way
I cannot eat, just want to sleep
My head is full, I start to weep
Instead of up I'm spiraling down
I've had enough I might just drown
Then comes a voice from deep within
You can't give up don't let it win
My fight goes on inside my head
Do I move on or just stay in bed
Some days are easy others not
Today is one that's best forgot

Just Surviving *by Marcia Durant*

I sit and stare into the darkness
Things unseen are always troubling
Struggling to escape the harshness
My thoughts seem to be crumbling
Another day on earth to survive
Sometimes I need to simply hide
Today's a good day to be alive
But tomorrow I may awake terrified
Promise of hope around the corner
One more day and things seem brighter
Not making anyone become a mourner
Exhausting most days just being a fighter

SCARS *by Marj O'Neill-Butler*

The monologue SCARS is based on the last year of the pandemic and the time I watched my husband's brain begin to unravel. Character: a woman 60+, any race or ethnicity, any size or shape.

The first scar I got was at Girl Scout Camp. I was running and tripped on a big root. Damn that hurt. Taken to the doctor outside of camp. Left knee, big messy scar.

Many years later C-section. Twice. Those don't show unless I'm naked. And I got two beautiful boys out of them. Then years after that one knee replacement. Three hip replacements. I don't care who sees these scars.

Aging, aging. I really am like the bionic woman. But, I stand tall. I work out. I live life to the fullest.

I also have mental scars. Things that have been said to me and about me. It's amazing how things like that stay with you. And those who love me have made those scars too. You have a flat ass. Where are your boobs? But you carry on. You try not to let them scar your life.

But recently, the deepest scar is in my heart. It crept up on me like many things. Odd behavior. Forgetfulness. Quirks that once seemed funny, no longer are. I don't know why I didn't spot things sooner. Maybe because I was not willing to give up on a wonderful relationship. He has been the love of my life. Tall, good looking with an open, friendly face. People have always taken to him. I literally swooned when I first set eyes on him. I thought to myself, who is that?
Clearly he thought the same. What fun to find someone like that after the age of fifty and a really contentious prior marriage.

Compatible doesn't begin to describe our relationship. We had a romping good time up until his stroke. That was almost two years ago. He tried his best to come back. Worked willingly in physical therapy. But what we didn't know then, was that the stroke had affected his brain as well. Slowly, slowly, things began to change. When you're with someone you love, you can forgive an awful lot.

So, I did. Put it down to aging. Or his sometimes weird ways. I loved the man. That's all. But as things got worse and worse and the man I knew started to disappear once in a while, I got concerned. What was this? Stop it. But he couldn't, of course. As bad days turned into weeks and months, my heart got heavier. It did. I could feel the ache in my chest from the weight.

Finally, he knew that he had to go into care. He saw me running everything. Doing everything. With no time for myself. For the last two months, I rarely wrote. I couldn't get my head around it. And I couldn't live uninterrupted. No matter how many times I discussed it with him, he would always break into my Zoom meetings with a mundane need or question.

I'm sure I looked like a harridan talking firmly to him with my sound off. Thankfully no one mentioned anything. Finally, I really wanted to listen to some monologues that had won a big contest. He couldn't let me get through that without needing something urgently. Like his iPad was broken. Or his computer was hacked.

Two days before he was to move into his studio apartment in assisted living, he started acting up so badly and so ferociously that I had to call 911. I was afraid of him because he started to get physical. This man who loved me tenderly and with such joy, was now kind of a monster. A lot of things happened that week that still shake me to my core. Finally on the drive north, I prayed we would get there without incident. My hands gripped the wheel so tightly, they hurt. When I left him, he was resigned and quite calm. I can't say the same for myself. I could barely drive home. I was crying so much.

Living alone after such a delicious marriage has been a challenge. I yearned for some peace. Some time to myself. Couldn't wait for him to go. But then, there I was alone in a big house feeling the emptiness. I doubt I'll ever get over this time in my life. It hurts so badly.

It's like a death really. The mischievous twinkle he always had in his eyes is gone. They are dead now, his eyes. Blank stare. I wonder where he's gone? How he sees things? He would hate to see himself like this. He was always so open and kind and affectionate. Now it's like looking at a dead man. What is that expression? A dead man walking? That's my husband.

I have scars all over my body. But there's one that's not visible. But no matter how much time passes, it still hurts. My heart is scarred for life.

Wharton Creek *by Michael Strosahl*

Lay me down
in the meadow grasses,
where we once lost ourselves
listening to the gurgle
of Wharton Creek.
Cover me with
Black-eyed Susans,
gathered in bouquets.
Stay a while
and tell me stories
of the beautiful world you see
though bright eyes.
Mine were always
too dark.

You do not remember
the day I was born,
the day he declared his love
with gifts and kind words,
then tore into my panties,
pushing his thick fingers
there.
You escaped
to the tall green grass,
while I kept
screaming for mommy,
and he
pressed his hand
over my mouth
for silence.

My,
how you have grown
by these waters,
but you always let me play,
dancing among the wildflowers
as you stared
through empty years,
searching for the secret
I bore away.

You know now.
You do not need me anymore,
your black-eyed Susan,
the one playing hide-and-seek
with your memories,
peeking out
at the most
inopportune times.
It is time for you
to face life full-on,
complete.

So lay me down
in these tall meadow grass,
where we once lost ourself.
Let me listen to the waters,
and maybe even
to a story from you
once in a while,
one of that beautiful world
you have come to know
beyond Wharton Creek.

Recounting the Scars *by Michael Strosahl*

This one is from
a rock I threw,
not expecting ricochet,
and I remember,
with no one around
I let the tears flow.

That one down there
was a wild ride
on my banana seat Stingray,
pedaling furiously until
kicking out my back tire,
throwing rocks from tread—
only once
it bucked me
and I flew,
touching down
without landing gear
into the gravel
we would pick from the wound
for days.

This one bled
from shattered glass,
and as I pulled the shards free
I noticed my eyes
were clear and dry.

Those,
those were self-inflicted
the day she left and
tore my soul apart,
just stabbed me deep
and walked away,
my heart tossed
into the corner wastebasket
as she closed the door behind her—
I wanted my blood to follow.

Which leads me to this one,
pulsing with every beat,
the one that has
ripped open so many times
I believe it to be
more scar than birthed flesh.
I know
it will bleed again
the day you leave.
And I will clean away the debris,
apply antibiotic to the new gash,
bandage it up real nice
so that it will heal once again
covered with
yet another permanent reminder,
a bump maybe,
or a discolored line
that I will someday
explain to someone else
as my eyes remain tear-free

and I will feel nothing.

Good Riddance & Goodnight *by Mikayla Cyr*

Nouns seem to come and go
People, places, things
Ebbing around the edges of
Our shorelines after they
Storm the sands of our souls
We honor the tides by giving them the space to drift in
And out of our grasp
Giving away to the colors of
Fading light and falling dark
To paint a portrait of what's
Meant to be
What should be

I haven't been hurt quite
Badly enough to learn that
Playing with fire isn't
Worth the burns
But I have been battered down
Low enough to grow afraid of
Feeling anything but the cold
And if this eager heart could
Keep warm on its own
What will it take for me
To see that distance doesn't mean safety
Let alone satisfaction

Love was never designed
To be supplied in fractions
And when mine becomes too much
Because you've grown accustomed
To bits and pieces out of convenience

I'll simply ask you to go find less
If my abundance is your downfall
I will not grow smaller to save you
I will not become a haunted garden
Of decayed dreams and bouquets
Of bloodshed to fit your description

I've lived far too long with
This cemetery mouth
Learning how to resurrect the
Words and feelings I let die
Before they had the chance to
Pass my lips and come to life
I'm becoming one with the flesh
That's held me together
And learning how to say goodbye
To the moments that weren't sure
Of how to greet me when we met
So on that note, I bid you
Good riddance
And goodnight

Eviction Notice *by Mikayla Cyr*

This is an eviction notice
To the demons that have
Squatted in my bones for
Longer than tides have
Kissed shorelines
I'm a heathen but I've done
All I can to ask for forgiveness
And I won't lie down and die
To let an invisible disease take
Me out with its bare hands
Explosions of anhedonia
Like lifeless fireworks
Booming unsaturated
I didn't sign up for this
Invisible show of lights
I didn't ask for a melancholy
Macabre state of mind
And I damn sure never once
Put up a sign asking
for roommates or tenants
Especially for those who don't pay
Rent and always fucking rob me
I am taking back my body
I am taking back my mind
I am fighting to the death
To take back what is mine
Sweating out the sins and
Picking myself up off the floor
Sweeping out the sadness and
Taking the hinges off the doors
This is an eviction notice

For a devilish unwelcome overstayed
Faucets left running and debts unpaid
Heed this warning and
Read the note carefully
Get the hell out and
Don't come back.

Show & Tell *by Mikayla Cyr*

Growing up far too fast
Forced walls painted of gray
Kidnapped childhoods
and unfinished lists
Dissipated opportunity
faded into chilling mist
Living inside pockets
made of holes
Gingham squares
And generational gaps
Lapses in judgement
like lilac season
Nothing lasts long
Let alone forever
Losing sight of purpose
in cascading years and
fistfuls of soot - the
fluorescent residue of
leftover lunch meats
Stinging on my tongue
Chewing on the stars
like a candle thrown
across a disheveled room

The same hands that tried to
keep themselves warm were
the cold fingers snapping
my bra strap against
contradicted consent

Convoluted upwind
battles in downstream
clichés of evolution
Cursed curves to a body that
became phosphorescent litanies
through time and space
to the same grown children
Now begging for a taste
of softness in a handful
Intrinsic impulsivity created
reactionary volatility
Time never prepared
me to write that story
Esoteric field days for
over-analytical hoarders
of thoughts
Like junkies of resolve
condemning the pain
with the flavor of
forget-me-nots
Forget her not
Survival of the fittest
wasn't a choice
But the rejection of losing a
battle she never asked to fight
Bee stings and broken glass
were the cradle of hope she built
That pieces can break and still be
beautiful without scrambling or
splintering hands forcing them
back together
Time is an open wound that
offers bandages in the form
of newer, stronger parts

Ones made of titanium and
hard-candy coatings
But who's going to write
a story about that

A Pain She Paints With Poetry *by Ndaba Sibanda*

he says a poem that shines a light
on her tenderness is a delight
she says a piece that pieces
together the intricacies
of their union
is a canyon

an ache she can't dislodge
is an infinite and unseen gorge
whose river patters, pours with passion
into her like a cloud that carries an abrasion
she claims that there is sweet poetry in her pain
that drives her hurt heart to prance like a pounding rain

A Healing Heart *by Ndaba Sibanda*

inner beauty is priceless
its twinkle is taintless
its hoot is humankind
its love is one of a kind

inner beauty is invaluable
its splash & sparkle, silent & able
it is an oak wood which is yielded
from the solidest timber ever preserved

in general, it provides trust, temperature
moderation & is prized for real furniture,
groundwater recharge, water pollution
attenuation & air pollution reduction

like an oak tree, its heart is harvested
& invested in humanity, it's cultivated
to weather moisture, rotting and decay
during different seasons & times, I say!

butted by lost winds & earths that are unclean,
inner beauty remains shiny, solid & evergreen,
it grows both in temperate & tropical climates,
a handsome heart heals medical ailments & mates

Kindling And Kind Heart *by Ndaba Sibanda*

her heart is a hefty, happy hearth,
a fireplace blazes and plumps
the depths of her interior life
it glows and grows every day
as if fuelled and fanned
by some frantic firewood

The Rainbow *by Noel Arzola*

Red life spills from her body,

producing internal screams.

Her form is covered with thick, red feathers.

They fall off, leaving deep scars.

Orange creatures hover overhead,

protecting and guarding her broken heart.

She receives a scroll from one of the birds.

Upon reading its contents, she cringes at the warning of its hopeful

message.

Yellow roses bloom in the glaring sunlight.

The promise of spring is a mockery.

Its cheerful distractions taunt her soul.

She is unable to shed the feelings of betrayal.

Green leaves quiver against the wind.

She is reminded of the green peridot that would have been given to her

child,

had it been born.

Instead, she wears a heart-shaped peridot around her neck.

Blue skies torment her demeanor,

creating a chasm from the smile on her face and the sadness lingering

within.

The skies will fade into a winter's tale,

leaving icicles to pierce her once hopeful heart.

Indigo flowers bloom again in the spring.

They whisper to her, and she waters them with her tears.

She hides amongst them, protecting her secret.

Deep within the wilderness, she holds her breath.

Violet robes drape her being and hide the newly formed wings.

She is wearing her crown again.

Whispers of smoke rise above the ashes,

and the internal light shines from her eyes.

Nine months later she looks towards the sky,

as colors illuminate the expanse.

Gazing down, she finally breathes again.

She's holding the rainbow in her arms.

Together *by Pratibha Savani*

I saw my mum for the last time today
We were together
Holding her hand
Chanting together
Hoping she could hear our sounds

She was calm
In a semi-comatose state
She was at peace
With her shallow breathing

We were there
'Til her very last breath
Tears were flowing
As our chanting grew louder
Creating a spiritual broadcast
For her celestial journey

I saw my mum for the last time today
Together we accepted her fate
Together we sang for the divine great
Together we knew our tears would gently fade away

Piercing Through the Black *by Pratibha Savani*

it is said....
there is light at the end of a tunnel
   we don't see it
      until....
   we are ready
   we are willing
   and we want to
   and the light comes
   like a light bulb moment
      hitting fast
      as you emerge out
   STRONGER
   WISER
      and EMPOWERED
   than ever before
   taking ALL that darkness
      you acquired
         piercing though....
      that wicked black
   and fighting back
      with ALL that might
   POWER
   so that the LIGHT
that RAINBOW
   is in your reach
   and you know it is
      cos you are already....

        THERE

Every Day is a Healing Day *by Pratibha Savani*

Every day is a healing day
That's what I have to keep saying
That's what I have to remember
That's what I have to do
I know it's true
Because every day is new
And every day moves forward
If you let it
So let it
Then every day is a healing day

Watercolors *by Rachel Leitch*

April 15, 1912

"Why don't you paint, Annabell?"

I twirled the paintbrush in my fingers and stared hard at the set of watercolors on the table beside my wheelchair. Waited for the images to swirl through my mind like a mystical fairy, a muse that poured from my imagination through my fingers into my paintbrush.

Nothing came. Maybe it never would again. And the end of never was much closer today than it had been yesterday.

I threw the paintbrush down on the table harder than I had intended. Because it frightened me how much I had intended it.

My brother, Benjamin, sank onto the edge of my bunk. "You always said painting made things clearer."

A twinge of guilt rippled through my stomach with another rumble from outside. Icebergs, the steward had said. Nothing to worry about. A common occurrence in this stretch of waters.

The Titanic was indestructible.

But I wasn't, and the ice in my mind was far more worrisome. It wasn't fair to Benjamin. He shouldn't be stuck inside this cabin with me when we were sailing on one of the finest ships in the world. He'd missed out on so much because of his sick little sister. For years. I clenched my fist around the paintbrush. None of this was fair.

Benjamin's voice swam. "If it truly makes things clearer, then maybe I should take up painting myself."

I should tell him he could have my things. But my throat hurt too much. And somewhere deep inside me, the words weren't true. Not just yet.

If I had only one wish, I'd turn back time so we never boarded this boat. Never set out on this journey. Never got the specialist's opinion. We had all thought the visit would heal my illness. Fine sea air and a specialist's opinion—how could it not?

Deep down, I knew changing the past wouldn't change anything. I was still dying. Three months, at the best. But perhaps it would have been better, happier not to know. To live out the rest of my days blissfully unaware that they were the final ones.

Benjamin clenched his fingers around the edge of the canvas. "It wasn't supposed to happen this way."

I tucked the canvas back in the drawer. "I can't paint. There's just . . . nothing there." The words felt sluggish on my tongue. There had always been something there. I painted when I couldn't go to the parties and picnics the other girls my age did. When I couldn't even go to school for how sick I was. My imagination was always there.
A rumble ominously echoed my words, and this time I felt the vibration ripple through the floor and into my wheelchair.

"It's been doing that for the past two hours. We could go see those icebergs the steward told us about," I suggested.

I didn't want to move. It was hard even to breathe. But when else was I going to have the chance to see something like this? When else would Ben have the chance to do something like this with me?

I was angry, but I wasn't sure at whom. Perhaps just myself, for being so whiny and selfish.

The door crashed open, and the steward Ben had befriended poked his head in. "Everyone in their life jackets and up to the main deck." I placed my hands on my wheels, preparing myself to push off. Ben gripped the handles of my wheelchair. "Is something the matter?" "Just a precaution. Excuse me while I wake the other cabins. I'll be back if you need any help with the chair." The door creaked closed.

It'd never creaked before.

A prickle of red-hot panic melted the ice in my mind. Immediately, I regretted wishing the ice would melt and wished instead that I could stay numb forever.

I pulled myself forward on shaky wrists and laid a hand on Ben's arm. He stared at the door as another rumble shook the ship. He shook false cheer into his voice. I knew what it sounded like, I'd heard it many times throughout my life, much of it my own. "You heard the man. Life jackets and up to the main deck. I suppose we'll be seeing those icebergs after all."

Ben pulled my life jacket from where I'd tossed it in the bottom drawer. I hadn't imagined I'd ever need it. Nothing could sink her, they said. Apparently, they'd lied. Just our luck.

He fitted it over my dinner gown. I tried to push my wheelchair to the door, one of the few things I could still do to help, but my arms shook too much. My strength was slipping so fast.

Ben doubled back and yanked open one of my drawers.

"Benjamin, honestly!" It came out more snappish than I wanted. Most of my words seemed to be doing that these days.

He pulled out my newest set of watercolors, just purchased in Southampton, where this wretched journey began. Then he pulled out a canvas from the furthest corner—a painting I'd done of that very city as our ship pulled in.

Why was he doing this? Unless he thought . . .

Unless he thought we wouldn't be back.

I tried to push the watercolors and canvas back at him. If we were packing, there were far more important things we could take with us.

"You don't need to—"

Ben pressed the watercolors and canvas back in my lap. He flung open the door and pushed my chair out into the passageway.

People sprinted up the ladder to the deck without a care for anyone or anything else. One mother dragged her child straight into my wheelchair. A surge of irritation bubbled up in me. The child was grinning as if this were all a grand adventure. No one in particular seemed very worried. If we got to the deck, and this was all a drill . . . Ice laced Ben's breath as he lifted my chair.

A gentleman bumped us with his suitcase on his own charge up the ladder. Ben lost his grip and we both tumbled to the floor. The gentleman never once glanced back.

I gripped the arms of my wheelchair as pain surged through my neck and back.

"You alright?" Ben ran his hands over my head.

I ducked gently away from his hands and nodded.

Ben took the paints and canvas back, lifted me from the chair, and sprinted up the ladder before someone else could bowl us over.

My chair clattered, abandoned behind us.

Our charge ended in a wall of people. Everyone seemed to be moving, but no one seemed to be going anywhere. Stewards scurried about. Crew members examined instruments I'd never seen before, tugged on ropes, clambered up and down ladders. And always the people pushed and shoved . . .

I drew my arms in as tight next to myself as I could, feeling very small. "Ben, what do you see?" I craned my neck. For the first time, I realized we stood at an angle.

Not us . . . The ship rested at an angle. Something was horribly wrong. "The women and children are boarding lifeboats." The frozen breeze frisked his hair as he gazed down at me. "That means you."

"No, Ben. We stay together." I clutched at his lapels. "I can wait for another boat."

He laid the paints and canvas in my lap. "It's only for a little while." "Then I can wait with you. Put me down."

Ben kicked and elbowed his way to one of the lifeboats in time with my protests. He laid me in the seat next to a woman with a sodden feather in her hat.

Ben looked past my shoulder to her. "Take care of her, please. Until I come back."

The woman pressed trembling lips together and nodded.
I wouldn't let go. I couldn't let go. This wasn't real. It couldn't be. Was this what dying felt like?

"Cut the ropes!" bellowed a crew member.

"Ben, come quickly, now!" I tugged on his coat.

But Ben only pried my hands free. "Soon, Annabell. Soon."

The lifeboat lurched, then plunged downward. Splash! Freezing water soaked my hair, coat, and canvas. I fought back a gasp, dabbed the canvas with my sleeve, and wrapped my arms tighter around myself for what little comfort that might provide.

And there we remained. The sailors rowed us away from the remains of the ship, but after that, we could do nothing more than row in circles—I could do nothing more than clutch the canvas to my chest and try not to cough too hard.

It seemed like minutes. It seemed like hours.

At last, the RMS Titanic tipped at a full angle, scattered people and objects into the water. It held its position for one eternal moment, then slipped beneath the icy waves.

And Ben slipped with it.

The colors bled.

###

The steward assigned to make sure I could get from one deck to another safely must have forgotten I was still down here in my cabin. That was fine. He had a million things to do, I was sure. He had much to do for a regular voyage, much less picking up dozens of stranded survivors in lifeboats.

I didn't want to watch as we pulled into New York City anyway. A cough shuddered deep inside me as I pulled the canvas away from my chest. The surface had dried, but I knew the layers beneath were still damp, even if I couldn't feel it. It smelled like sea water, and not in a pleasant way.

No matter how it dried, I could never repair it. I couldn't even make out that Southampton dock from oh so long ago.

I didn't remember. Didn't care to.

We'd circled for hours, until the cold air and sea spray had invaded every fiber of my being. The ship's doctor had diagnosed me with pneumonia, and it had only worsened my illness.

Finally, a rescue ship came. Too late.

They never found Ben.

I wished we'd never left that dock in the painting. If Ben hadn't been escorting me to see the specialist, he would have never been on that boat. This was my fault.

Father and Mother were losing both their children because of me. If only I had been lost to the water instead of him. I was going to die anyway. It should have been me. I should have held on longer, insisted louder. If he wouldn't listen, I should have thrown myself back onto the ship and refused to move.

But I hadn't had the strength. And now Ben was gone.

A steward took the stairs two at a time and seemed surprised to see me. "I'm so sorry, miss! I didn't realize you were down here." He grabbed the handles of my wheelchair and headed for the stairs.

I forced a smile. "It's alright. I could have called out."

"But you're missing the view." He carried the chair up to the main deck and pushed my new wheelchair down the gangplank.

All around me people dashed off the ship, embraced their families, sobbed at their loss, laughed at their good fortune.

I scanned the crowd for a familiar face. Once, twice. Three times. No one stood there for me. Father and Mother were late.

The way things had been recently, I would have been frustrated. Angry, even. Now I just felt . . . nothing.

The canvas bled against my chest.

The steward left me on the pier across from a young woman not far from my own age. She wrung her hands in the most aggravating manner and stretched up on her tiptoes.

I followed her gaze until I saw what had so enraptured her.
A young man, not far off of Ben's age. Ben. . .

He ran towards the nervous young woman and caught her in his arms. She mumbled against his shoulder and laughed so hard she cried.

I turned away. Once more, I pulled the canvas away from my chest.

Bruised colors smeared against my fingertips.

I tossed the canvas into a pile of crates.

###

"Why don't you paint, Annabell?"

Ben's question. Mother's voice.

I couldn't find the words to answer. Only stared out the window in the same manner that I used most of my time as of late. The world went on beneath me in a brilliant rehearsal for how it would in three short months when I no longer joined its dance.

I was being horrible and selfish, I knew it. I couldn't find the words to explain how dull and gray the world was. How hard it was to even open my eyes in the morning. I loathed myself.

Mother gave up. I didn't blame her. "I'm going to grab another book from the library. Do you want anything?"

I worked up the will to shake my head. I didn't want anything that she was able to grant me.

She ran her hand across my forehead, a gesture that I couldn't imagine any judgement into even if I tried, then stepped out of the room.

I leaned my head against the back of my wheelchair.
Only moments passed before footsteps pattered in. The maid's footsteps, not my mother's.

My voice was barely a whisper. "Marion, I don't want anything. Please leave."

"Finally, I've found you!"

The voice most certainly did not belong to Marion. I dropped the hand from my eyes and turned as best I could.

I needn't have bothered. The footsteps brought a boy of ten in tattered clothes to stand in front of me. He carried a bulky cloth-wrapped object under his arm. He looked as out of place in this fine parlor as a mouse or some other such creature might.

He smelled like the sea. But I couldn't make out enough of the scent to decide whether it was in a pleasant way or not.

"Forgive me for sneaking past the maid, but I've been looking for you for months!" A grin lit up his freckled face, like the lights from the Carpathia had lit up the waters. Those lights hadn't been half as bright as his smile, though.

I laid my head back once more, just because it tired me too much to keep it upright. "I don't believe I'm who you're looking for."
"No mistake! See, your signature, right here." The boy tore the cloth off the object to reveal a canvas.

My canvas.

"May not be able to do much, but I can read. I had a time of it deciphering the signature, since it was so smeared and all. Suppose it must have gotten soggy in those crates. But I waited for it to dry, and now . . ." He set the canvas in my lap. "Here."

I didn't touch the canvas for fear it would crumble in my hands. The wounded colors wept even more in the sight of day. "I'm sorry you went to so much trouble for this piece of trash."

He looked at me in horror. "No, no, miss. It's not trash. It's too beautiful to be trash."

I stared down at the bleary canvas. A drop of orange graced the corner. Like a spark. Like a light from a rescue ship.

"I guess God hadn't finished it." With a wise little bob of his head, he brushed his hands together. "Well, I'm off."

"Wait." I brushed his arm and fumbled for my purse. "Please. Let me reward you."

He frowned and stepped back out of my grip. "But I didn't come for a reward." He scrunched up his face. "Finish the painting. That'll be a good reward."

He gazed at the blur of colors. And I let myself do the same. The colors sprang to life. Little pinpricks at first that burst from the dull gray. It hurt, like stepping into the sun with a headache. But only at first. And the longer I sat and let the colors surround me, it hurt just a little less.

I tucked my purse away. "Very well, then. So I shall."

He grinned wide enough to reveal a missing tooth.

"Would you do something for me? Let Marion know to bring my watercolors up."

"Straightway, miss." He tipped his cap and scurried away. I couldn't push my chair to the window, wasn't strong enough anymore, but I craned my neck just in time to watch him skip down the street towards the docks.

"Your paints, miss."

"Thank you, Marion." I dipped my brush into the cup of water. I lingered over each color I dripped the water into. Where to start? What to paint?

Marion was so kind as to bring up my easel as well. I set the canvas atop it and pulled my wheelchair closer.

I looked at the canvas. I looked at my palette. Did I even know where to start anymore?

Of course I did.

I dabbed my brush in the sky blue. Ben's favorite. I brushed it across the canvas with a shaking hand. It wasn't a particularly good stroke, but it was something.

I followed it with a streak of lilac, my personal favorite. The feeble strokes bled together into the sky beyond my window.

Perhaps God hadn't finished after all. Today, I wasn't alright. It still hurt. And maybe it'd still hurt tomorrow. But maybe it would hurt a little less, a little different. And one day, maybe it would be a sweet hurt. Maybe.

I turned a corner of my mouth up. "Yes, Ben. I'd love to paint."

Back to the Drawing Board *by Rachel Leitch*

1942, Hollywood, California

"Um, excuse me?" Tap, tap, tap.

I darkened the eye of a snarling dog and rolled my eyes upward. "Yes?"
"Sorry." The dark-haired man invading my cubicle held out one
smudged hand. "To interrupt, I mean."

I closed my sketchbook.

He nodded towards it ever so slightly. "I'm supposing you're not a
secretary here, then."

First rookie to recognize that. I supposed I ought to offer him a hand
to shake. "I'm Retta Shaw. An animator."

He shook it in one quick jerk and shifted his weight to his right foot.
"I'm Wolfgang Schulze. Uncle Walt, uh, Mr. Disney's nephew? Looks
like I'll be working here for a while."

He glanced around my office. Funny how a room that had looked the
same for three years now could be completely new to someone
else—the framed illustration of Snow White, the faded engagement
photo in the corner of my desk, the beaded lamp to its opposite
Wolfgang palmed his forehead. "This is your office. I should have
known."

I waited for an explanation.

He tried to laugh, but he must not have tried it in a while. "It is funny.
Really. The other animators told me this would be my office."

Of course. I shouldn't have been surprised. But I was still disappointed, which was surprising in its own right.

Wolfgang pushed a sprig of dark hair behind his ear, but it sprang back.

"I guess they just don't like rookies."

"No." I scooped up a stack of papers and sketchbooks and memorandums from the smaller desk along the back wall. I used it mostly for storage, which really meant whatever half-finished drawings I wasn't working on at the time. I dumped the stack into the overflowing bottom drawer in my main desk. "They just don't like me."

"Oh." Wolfgang twisted his hands around the strap of his satchel. "Trust me. A dozen rookies have marched in here believing it was their office." A stack of papers tumbled to the floor and the drawer bumped shut.

"Don't worry." He set the stack back on the table. "I'll hide out somewhere else until they can find me an office that doesn't have someone else's name attached."

I set the stack of papers right back in the drawer. "Please. It's no trouble. This table needed cleared off anyways. Can't imagine why I hadn't done it before now."

A wonder he hadn't gotten his finger stuck in that twisted strap by now.

"If you're certain."

"I think I am." I shoved the drawer closed. "Here. Get yourself settled and I'll check in with Mr. Disney. See about getting you the real deal."

"No, please don't do that."

"Why not?"

He shifted his weight again. A nervous habit, then. He seemed to have a lot of those. "I made myself a bet. That I could make my way here without begging to Uncle Walt."

"Then it's good you're not begging. Neither am I. I detest begging." I turned on my heel in a pivot that might have made my husband Stephen's general proud and strode down the hall to Mr. Disney's office.

I stared hard at the other animators' offices as I strode by—all male animators, I might note. Marc didn't even try to hide his smirk, a smirk that wavered too much to be real.

I rapped on Mr. Disney's door and glanced back just in time to see Marc's smirk morph into something as steady as a line from a toddler's pencil.

"One moment, Retta."

I always knocked the same way, so no surprise he knew it was me. I glanced in the mirror, patted a strand of brown hair back into my bun, and straightened my checked dress. It was a little worn, but there hadn't been much extra money for frivolities lately. Or even for non-frivolities.

There was a war on, after all.

I'd never been much for frivolities, anyway.

Mr. Disney opened the door. "Retta! Have you finished the dogs already?"

"Not yet. But they're coming along fearsomely."

"As I knew they would."

My eyes discovered the half-drawn storyboards in the corner immediately. I lowered my voice. "We've opened production on Cinderella?"

Cinderella had always been my favorite fairy tale, long before I learned that fairy tales never quite came true the way they do in cartoons. I'd pushed for the film in meeting after meeting, but the male animators thought we were better off continuing to work on live action films with cartoon addendums.

Disney waved his hand. "Rough storyboards."

"I know someone who wouldn't mind drawing the lead model." What was I doing? Just avoiding the matter at hand, that was what.

He raised his eyebrows with a grin. "Noted." He perched on the edge of his desk. "But you didn't come here just to remind me of that again." I mimicked him on a table. Of course, he'd bring me back where I was supposed to be. "Wolfgang." It was the only word I could get out. This had all seemed so clear in my head earlier.

"On his first day?" Disney outlined Donald Duck on a crumpled napkin. "Can't help but love the lad, but he finds himself in the strangest predicaments." His chuckle afterward made it seem far from a laughing matter. As if Wolfgang were a sad situation altogether. What did he mean by that?

"He hasn't. Not purposely. The other animators sent him to my office, with the understanding that it was his office."

Disney set down his pencil.

I rocked my foot on the heel of my scuffed black oxfords. "This, ah, isn't the first time this has happened."

For once, Disney's hands were still. "I wish you had spoken up sooner." I pinched the folds of my dress. "Perhaps I should have."

But perhaps I was a bit like Wolfgang. When Mr. Disney had been so kind as to give me this job, I'd made a bet with myself that I wouldn't go whining to him every time I didn't get my way. I'd work harder than any of the men here. And it had served me well thus far, although it had not helped in winning over the other animators.

Disney's voice sliced off my thoughts. "But today, I am to blame. I sent Wolfgang to your office."

My oxford slipped off my foot. I barely caught it, even as a tiny flare of something else caught in my chest. Did Disney even think so lowly of me?

"Not to insult you. We simply don't have any more offices. Wolfgang just walked in and asked for a job. He needed the job."

Something about the way he emphasized needed made me pause.

"The other animators would poke and prod him until he gave up any artiste that he may or may not have. But you wouldn't. And right now, he needs that artiste."

I took a deep breath in and let it out quietly, a practice Stephen had taught me for when I was feeling irritated. Flying into a passion wouldn't help anything.

Disney glanced back at a set of files that seemed rather drab compared to the cartoons hanging about the office. "We already have more workers than we can pay. The war has changed things."

Yes, it had. So many things. Things that didn't need to be changed. Stop thinking about that.

"If things continue . . . I may have to lay off." He looked at me too long with a too worried frown.

Not me. I couldn't get laid off. I couldn't go back home with nothing, not after the whole family had made a holiday of warning me against this job.

Women don't draw cartoons.

They'll cast you out as soon as the war is over and the men come back. It's not a ladylike profession.

I couldn't go back to their busy noisy house where everything went on as it always did, but neither could I go back to my own home where nothing went on.

I bit my lip. "I understand. We'll make the best of it."

"Thank you, Retta."

I straightened my skirt. "Back to the dogs I go." And Wolfgang. Who wasn't a dog, but still.

When I returned to my office, Wolfgang had folded his lanky frame into the storage table and bent over his own papers. Had Disney given him assignments already? Perhaps nephew-ship helped with that.

I bee-lined for my desk. I'd learned fast to do it every time I walked in the room. I'd still never found an animation of Donald Duck that had vanished after Marc was in my office for a meeting.

But this time, my sketchbook remained closed. None of the papers in the drawers had been rifled through. No fingerprints smudged on the picture frame.

Even those who had no ill intent had never left my things alone. Curiosity always overcame them.

I dusted the picture frame off anyway. I stacked the papers and knickknacks in a spare chair. Then I grabbed one corner of my desk and dragged it across the rug. It screeched so loud Frank probably heard it in his office on the second floor.

Wolfgang whipped around in his seat, with a look on his face that I could only describe as terror. But why?

"Sorry." I kept dragging with as much speed and as little screech as possible. Which was not very much at all.

With what seemed to be considerable effort, his face relaxed. His shoulders, however, did not. "What are you doing?" He crossed the office—with a decided limp, I noticed—grabbed the other corner of my desk, and helped me bump it to its final resting place.

"I like being able to see everyone in a room." I smoothed my hair and rolled my desk chair into place.

Wolfgang handed me my photo. "You don't trust many people, do you?"

"I just like to know what's going on." I returned it to its place of honor.

145

Wolfgang handed me my corkboard next. "Nice wings."

I took the corkboard with barely a glance towards the pair of US Air
Force wings pinned to the board beside my day's assignments.
He shifted his weight once more, then returned to his desk.
I blew out one last long breath, settled in my seat, and pulled my
sketchbook from the drawer.

Wolfgang dragged his desk chair to the backside of his table.

I waited for an explanation.

"I like knowing what's going on, too." He gave me a salute, but his
hand shook. He folded back into the chair, and resumed scribbling.
Hmm. Perhaps this Wolfgang wouldn't be so bad after all.

Perhaps.

###

My pencil gashed in dark lines over the dog's back. I squeezed my eyes
closed, tried to see the dogs, waited for them to come alive in my mind
as they always did.

But today they didn't.

I still had to draw all the animation frames for them. I had to finalize
the design this week, no exceptions. I couldn't give Disney any reason
to lay me off.

Different tactic. I imagined the animations of Bambi that a remarkably
apologetic Marc had shown me yesterday. Then I pictured my dogs
behind Bambi.

The dogs snapped, snarled, slobbered to life.

But they weren't chasing Bambi. They were chasing Stephen, as he looked in the photo on my desk. And they weren't dogs. They were German soldiers.

No. Not this again.

"What do you think?"

My eyes flew open with a gasp.

Wolfgang startled, jerking his chair back. He recovered and rolled his desk chair precisely three inches closer to mine and no further. "I'm sorry. I didn't mean to startle you."

I rubbed my eyes. I grabbed the drawings of the dogs and stuffed them in the top drawer. Perhaps I'd gotten as far as I could on them. Right now I didn't want them anywhere near me.

I took Wolfgang's drawing carefully so I didn't smudge it. It felt good to have something busying my hands.

A skunk in a meadow, in the typical Disney style. Fuzzy white stripes and big blue eyes. I hadn't found skunks cute since one had sprayed Stephen on our first anniversary. Was everything destined to remind me of him today?

As if it didn't do that every day.

I couldn't help but love Wolfgang's skunk, though. "That's really good."

"Meet Flower." Wolfgang displayed her like I imagined Michelangelo had the Mona Lisa.

"Brilliant."

Wolfgang set his drawing aside. "Do you mind if . . . I could see yours?" Wolfgang had always stayed at his desk and I had stayed at mine. Mostly. But he kept his nose out of my drawings and I kept my nose out of his.

Still . . . he had asked nicely.

I slowly opened the drawer. Nothing leapt out at me. "You can't pass on the design to anyone," I said, more to cover this strange anxiety than of an actual fear that he'd sell me out.

"Why would I do that?" Wolfgang fidgeted with the strap of the messenger bag over the back of his chair.

I passed him the drawing so I wouldn't have to look. But I looked anyway.

The whole group of them teemed into a frenzy of blacks and browns. Some boasted beady green eyes, others deep dark ones. Their mouths stretched wide, their teeth snapped.

"These dogs chase Bambi, right?"

"So says master storyboard." I bit my lip. "I was going for terrifying but not too terrifying." That made even less sense when it came out of my mouth.

"Wow. That's intense."

"Is that bad?"

"No. Can you imagine when these blast on the screen?" He laid the papers down. "It'll be a story no one ever forgets."

That no one ever forgets. Retta Scott and her art would not be forgotten. No matter what any gloom-and-doom predicted. "Thanks."

"If you can draw like this, why don't you draw lead model?"

"Haven't gotten there yet, I guess." I turned back to my drawing board.

"Do you ever get tired of drawing something scary?"

"No. We need to know scary things are out there. And we need to know how to fight them." I stuck my pencil between my teeth as I arranged the papers.

Wolfgang tilted his head. "Sage words from a veteran dog-fighter?"
I nodded and pushed the dogs back into a drawer.

Wolfgang picked at a loose thread on his bag. "Same here."

###

"Retta, what do you think of the different texture I gave Flower's tail?"
I shook the dogs from my mind and glanced over his drawing. I tapped a red fingernail on it. I'd originally settled on red because it seemed patriotic. Now it just seemed like blood. "Send that to ink and paint right now."

"That good?"

"Of course!" I turned back to my drawing board and waited for Wolfgang's chair to scoot back.

But it didn't.

I turned back around, anxiety knotting my stomach. "Did you need something else?"

"I don't mean to pry, but, I've been meaning to ask . . . who's this?" Wolfgang kept his finger a respectable distance back from the picture frame.

Part of me had hoped he would ask. But now that he had . . . "Me." He rolled his eyes.

"My husband, Stephen."

"Oh." He leaned back in his chair. "How long have you been married?" I drummed my pencil against the desk. Please stop asking questions.

"Would have been two years."

Wolfgang clenched his hands in his lap. "The war?"

I pressed the pencil against the desk, hard enough it cracked. I stared down at the splinters. "I should have never let him climb in that airplane. He said it'd all be over soon, that he'd come back."

"I'm sorry." He traced his toe across the floor. "I was there. It's . . . horrible."

I tilted my head, not much unlike Flower did in his many sketches. He rubbed his kneecap. That silence stretched between us for too long.

Maybe he didn't want to talk about it either.

I turned back to my desk to relieve the tension.

Wolfgang took a shaky breath. "I wanted to die."

His voice was the smallest whisper I'd ever heard. I almost wasn't sure I'd truly heard it.

I laid one hand on his arm, the only thing I knew to do. "I did, too." He gently pulled the broken pencil from my hands. And I let him. I stood in a rush that spilled pencil shavings on the floor and made Wolfgang jump. I grabbed one corner of my desk and dragged it around, screech by screech.

Wolfgang pressed his hands to his ears, but I kept working. Until our desks were side by side.

Wolfgang rubbed a pencil shaving between his fingers, staring at the desks. "I thought it made you—"

I turned my chair so we were side by side. "Not with the right coworker."

A siren split the air between us.

Wolfgang flinched and curled tighter into his chair.

I wouldn't deny that my own pulse skipped a beat, but the sound invaded at least once every week. I closed the blinds in our office and flipped the lights off. "Everyone meets down in the basement."

Wolfgang hugged his knees, rocking back and forth, hands over his ears, murmuring to himself.

Oh, no. I laid a hand on his arm. "Wolfgang? Are you alright?" He flinched away from my touch with a startled gasp.

I drew my hand back. Clearly, that wasn't what he needed right now. The siren wailed on in the background. I knelt so that I was on Wolfgang's level, but kept a few feet back. Hopefully, that gave him enough space. "You're going to be alright, Wolfgang. It's just a drill. Just for practice. It's not real."

Slowly, his hands fell away from his ears.

What had he seen? What had he experienced? What was hiding in his mind, waiting for the perfect opportunity to spring out and torment him?

I knew what he was feeling. Oh, how I knew.

I just had the good fortune of being a step or two ahead. For the first time, I wondered why.

As if someone had snapped their fingers, the siren stopped. "There? You see. It's over. We can go back to work now."

Wolfgang still didn't say anything as I turned the lights back on and settled into my chair. My own legs were shaking and I couldn't imagine why.

"I'm sorry," came a hoarse whisper from the desk behind me.

I glanced over my shoulder. "Why? What do you have to be sorry for?" He forced a tight smile and turned back to his desk, bracing his head in his hands.

###

I gathered all the storyboards back into a neat orderly stack. "It looks good, Mr. Disney. Really excellent. Cinderella may just make animation history."

Disney grinned. "I know. Everyone has done some great work on this, to turn it into a reality."

"We really do have a wonderful team."

"And I was thinking it might be a good time to make a certain someone a lead animator."

I dropped the stack of storyboards. "Are you . . . truly?"

"Why wouldn't I choose you?" Disney crossed his feet on his desk. "I think it's a good idea, and so does every other artist and animator in this building that I've asked."

They'd all stood behind me? Really? "I . . . Thank you!" I gathered up the papers, a wave springing loose from my bun.

Disney just shook with laughter.

I cleared my throat and tried to regain some of my long-gone composure. "And what will I be drawing?"

"Sorry to say, but I haven't given you Cinderella, the lead model. But you at least get my favorite animal."

I hadn't smiled like this in . . . years! "The mice."

"There'll be quite the handful of them. All at your disposal."

My disposal. I still couldn't believe it. I'd done it. I was no longer Retta the fool, drawing herself to financial ruin, as my family assumed Stephen would have been so proud, even if he didn't always understand my artistic bent.

Wolfgang would be proud, too. Prouder, even.

An idea sketched itself in my mind.

No. I couldn't. Not now. I'd finally made it. This was my chance to show all those other animators that the small measure of trust they apparently had in me was not misplaced. I needed to do this on my own.

Or did I?

"Off with you! Back to your desk and the brilliance already tumbling about your mind!" Disney shooed me from the room.

"Actually . . ." I licked my lips and forced the words to come out. "I may have a better idea for the mice."

"What could be better than you?" Disney folded up the storyboard with a final smack.

I smiled brightly. "Wolfgang. He and I have found we work pretty well together. I was wondering if he could work on my team."
Disney rubbed a finger over his mustache, staining it with ink, then let out a long sigh.

My senses went on high alert. "What's wrong?"

He drummed his fingers on the windowsill. "I've had to start laying people off."

I didn't say anything. Couldn't say anything.

"There's not an office left in this building that has two people in it anymore. I spoke with Wolfgang earlier. Explained that I would be speaking with you about this opportunity later today, and that if you said yes . . ."

Then Wolfgang would have to go.

In an instant, I knew what needed to be done. I knew I might regret it later. Knew I'd shed some tears when it was all said and done.
But I knew it was what needed to be done, and that was all I needed to know.

Stephen would have agreed in a heartbeat.

I handed the storyboards back to Disney. "Give the job to Wolfgang."
"You've worked far too long for this. You deserve it more than anyone else in this building."

"Wolfgang needs it more. I have a family. And I've learned so much from when I first started here." I could go home. I'd be alright. It wouldn't be wonderful, but for the first time, I truly believed that I would be alright. "Wolfgang needs it more. And this is only temporary. Once the studio gets back on its feet, I can come back."

Disney shook his head. "I hate to see you give all of this up."

"I'm not giving up."

He let out a long sigh and clapped one hand on my shoulder. "I hate to see you go, Retta. But you'll land on your feet. If you're certain about this—"

"Which I am."

"Then let's go tell Wolfgang the news."

But when we rounded the corner, our office was empty. Only a yawning, monochrome emptiness. Wolfgang was gone.

I checked my desk. No note telling me he was in a meeting or off on an errand or getting us some lunch. I rummaged through the files Wolfgang had helped me organize the other day. There was a paper in the incoming folder.

But the sketch I pulled out wasn't mine.

It was a dark pencil sketch of an eagle soaring over a battlefield. In the corner, with rough dark strokes, there was an outline of a wounded soldier on the ground, blood seeping from his leg. Everything about the drawing was dark.

Except for the eagle.

Wolfgang. He'd left so I wouldn't have to choose.

I spun. "We have to find him. Now."

###

Disney led me to Wolfgang's apartment first. The entire city had gone to sleep, with only a few street lights blinking sleepily above us. I had to slow my pace so Disney could keep up.

Disney pointed, but I'd already spotted him.

A lone figure with a sketchbook perched on the fire escape above us.

156

I gripped the railing. "If you'll give me a moment."

Disney nodded and leaned against the apartment wall.

Slowly, carefully, I climbed the rickety stairs, all the way to the top where Wolfgang was sitting. He looked up with a sad smile as I stepped over a missing stair.

I sat next to him and said nothing. I wasn't really sure what to say, and for the first time in a long time, I didn't need to know.

He let out a pitiful laugh. "I can't go in."

I waited for an explanation.

"Can't go in there by myself." He tapped his toe on the floor beneath us.

"Do you want to talk about it?"

"Not really."

I nodded and twisted my hat in my hands. "I didn't want to talk about Stephen either. Until one day, someone asked. And then a couple weeks later, someone else asked. And a while after that, someone else asked. Not expecting an answer. Just showing they'd listen when I decided to tell." I licked my lips as the wind blew several strands of hair free of my bun. "One of those people was you."

Wolfgang clenched his hands around his sketchbook. "I know why you're here, and I'm not going to let you leave your dream because of me."

"That's good, because I won't let you let me, either. It's my choice." I lowered my voice to a whisper. "You need this job far more than I do right now."

"The job means nothing if . . . if you're not there to help me."

"Disney can't afford to pay both of us." A light slowly dawned in my mind. "So I'll ask to stay on without pay."

"You can't do that. You have a house to pay for."

"Don't tell me what I can and cannot do," I teased. "I'll move back in with my family for the time being. Or find a roommate. We'll figure it out, you'll see."

He let his eyes fall closed with a small sigh. "Why are you doing this for me?"

"Because someone did it for me, and that's the only reason I'm here." I bent my head to look him in the eye, even though he couldn't see me.

"I'm returning your favor."

He opened his eyes, staring down at his sketchbook. "No one's ever come for me before. When I've felt like this. When I was overseas, I laid for days in the middle of a ravaged field, screaming, begging for help, my leg torn open and bleeding."

My heart plummeted in my chest and my breath caught. Tears I'd never let myself cry caught behind my eyelids.

"No one came. I had to drag myself to the field hospital alone. The doctors all expected me to die. Once I was even well enough, I drew to keep myself sane." A lone tear slipped out and he let out a long sigh. "I just, sometimes it feels . . ."

"Like you're alone and wounded in that field, screaming with no one to hear you," I said softly. I wiped my eyes on the back of my sleeves. "We hear you. And truth be told, we're screaming right along with you."
He rolled a pencil in between his fingers. "How do you know we're going to be alright?"

I opened the sketchbook to a clean page. "Because I've got moments like these to remind me."

Shred of Reality *by Rachel Leitch*

It was truly an unremarkable moment. If anyone asked me to describe it to them, I wouldn't be able to do it.

Then it happened.

I was curled up in the window seat of our two story home in New York reading a novel and twisting a strand of my long brown hair when feeling washed over me. Not one specific feeling, but rather all of them at once.

Anger that burned from the pit of my stomach up into my throat.

Sadness that chilled beneath my skin.

Anxiety that wavered in the edges of my vision.
And excitement that trembled from my fingertips through the rest of my body.

As if I had never realized how numb I was before.

I closed my book, climbed up on my knees, and peered out at the busy street below. It carried on as it always did. People scurrying back and forth, in and out of shops. Some clutched shopping bags or cellphones, while others pushed their earbuds in tighter and danced to music no one heard.

No one seemed to feel the everything.

But I couldn't focus on anything else.

It was as if a guard rail curbing the edge of my mind had been removed. There were things outside my mind that I'd never realized were standing there. And I desperately wanted to say hello.

Beat by beat, the feelings ebbed away, and in their place pooled something cold and dark. A sense that something was horribly wrong. I knew the feeling well and had felt it many times. But this was different.

This time, there came a sense that I somehow had a way to fix it.

I left my novel on the window seat and trailed into the library next door. Father was muttering to himself and sighing quite a bit, enough that I almost changed course and returned to my room.

Was he still upset that I had asked if I could have my friend from school over? I didn't understand why he made such a production of it, and when I asked him to explain, he simply said I needed to learn respect.

I was afraid to approach him, a fear I'd never noticed before. Yet it had always been there, just out of my reach.

The sense of terribly wrong insisted I enter, so I did. I cleared my throat, but he didn't look up. I got the sense he was waiting for me to speak.

"Father?" It didn't seem right on my tongue.

His eyes darkened as he looked up from his book.
I laced my fingers together tightly. "Something's wrong, isn't it?"

He frowned. "What do you mean?"

I unclenched my hands and fidgeted with one of the strings on my hoodie. "Just a feeling,

I suppose."

He leaned forward in his chair. "What kind of a feeling?"

I shrugged. "An everything all at once feeling."

He scoffed a bit then. "What is that supposed to mean?"

I turned to go. It had been foolish, I supposed. "Nothing, I guess." Like most anything else I said when I stood in that library.

I returned to my book on the window seat, but I couldn't concentrate. That something-wrong feeling persisted. I wished it would simply go away. My day had been just fine before it got here.

But over a few minutes, the feeling morphed again. And this time I realized it didn't mean I should go talk to my father.

It was the sort of feeling when something's wrong and you know you can do something about it.

I didn't know what, though. I leaned my head against the cool glass and watched the people crossing below my window as if they would give me an answer.

They never had before, but there was always a first time.

The light changed, releasing a flood of pedestrians into the crosswalk. A tire squealed, but the sound was muted, as if I were underwater and the sound were a great distance away. As if in slow motion, I saw a cab with no intent of slowing headed straight for the crosswalk.

No.

Everything froze.

I caught my breath. But nothing moved. Nothing except me. As if I'd stepped into a painting.

I raised one hand shakily, but the scene around me didn't change. Like it was waiting for me to do something.

But what? I didn't even know what I had done to stop time, much less what I could do to restart it. What if I did it wrong and something terrible happened?

A tiny whisper flowed from my mind through the rest of my body. You know what to do. You can do it.

I stood up on the window seat and turned in a tight circle. I imagined it as it had been, focusing, concentrating, thinking harder and harder until I got it down to every last detail.

Except for one.

I moved the speeding cab into a parking place outside of a nearby bookstore. I imagined the car was parked, the engine off. I imagined a police car there, too, just for good measure.

Something creaked in the library next door. I glanced towards it.

Time restarted.

The people below went on their merry way, showing off their purchases and chattering away on their phones as if nothing had ever happened.

Outside the bookstore, the police officer stepped out of his car to scold the reckless driver.

I had stopped time, and then restarted it. Not only that, but I had changed reality.

Was this normal? No. Could everyone do this? Again, I felt the answer,

No. Or was it only me?

My bedroom door creaked behind me before I could hear the answer to my last question. I spun, brown locks sailing over my shoulder. Father stood in the doorway, watching me with the sort of stare that made me feel dirty, as if I'd dropped his favorite book in the mud and deserved a scolding.

How long had he been there? Did he know reality had been changed? Did any of those people below? They didn't seem to know.

And yet Father knew.

He closed the door behind him. "No one must know, Shi. If they knew certain people in their midst could control the very reality they live in, can you imagine how they would react?"

I very purposely didn't. I didn't need those visions of fear coming true before my eyes.

"And you can't use those powers again for any reason."

But I'd just found them. I wanted to know more. Wanted to know what they could do, what they should do. They could do so much good. I wanted to learn how to use them and where they came from.

I'd thought he would be happy for me. Want to learn alongside me. But instead he'd only come in here to scold me.

I knew better than to say any of that aloud.

"They're dangerous. You could do anything with them. Everyone uses things to their own gain. Sooner or later, you will hurt people."

A tiny prick of fear poked me. Was that true? Would I only hurt people if I used my powers? That police car. What if I had pulled it from a more important distress call?

I lowered my head, very purposely refused to look at the people below, and returned to my book.

Perhaps I had done something terrible. Shame washed over me. Father left my room at last. I sat and read until the end of my book. Anytime a wayward thought about mind or time or power or reality entered my mind, I dutifully shoved it away and returned to my novel. It had an unsatisfying ending, the sort that makes you immediately search for something else to read to cover up the disappointment of the first.

So I found my way to the library. With nothing to distract my mind, a thought slipped through.

Perhaps there were books on my powers in here.
After all, Father hadn't seemed surprised by my powers. Perhaps he already knew and had been researching.

Perhaps, perhaps, perhaps.

I walked along the shelves, keeping my hands to my sides. Normally, I'd run a finger along the spines, but today, all of me was trembling.

I feared Father coming in and seeing me like this. And I oughtn't to be afraid of him.

That feeling of something terribly wrong roared back, so I searched a little faster.

Many volumes I had simply taken for granted were gone, I slowly realized. I'd never paid them much mind, so I couldn't tell you the titles or the color of the covers. All I knew was that they were gone. And, as with most other things, I immediately wondered why. I know a way you can find out, a tiny voice inside me whispered. No. I couldn't. He'd expressly told me not to. He'd say I was being disobedient and reckless.

Maybe I was.

But I couldn't think of any earthly reason why I shouldn't try. I turned in a slow circle and imagined the library the way it had been only a couple days ago. Sure enough, books appeared in the empty slots. Once I'd restarted time, I pulled one of the missing books off the shelf. It was as solid as any of the others.

This wasn't just my imagination.

Where I had pulled the book out, it left a hole.

Not just a gap in the bookshelf, as one would naturally assume. But a hole in the wall.

A hole in reality.

The jagged edges of the hole shimmered with golden light. But how could that be? What was in here was real. This house was real. What I watched out my window every day was real.

Unless it wasn't.

What if I weren't the only one who could bend reality?
And what if the other one who could very much wanted me to stay
here?

My mind screamed that it wasn't true, it couldn't be Father. But
everything made sense now and I couldn't go back.

That was how he'd been able to give me whatever my heart desired for
so long. That was why I could never have any friends over and why he
disliked me associating with anyone else.

That was why he doted on me one second and seemed profoundly
disappointed in me the next, no matter what I did.

But why did he want me here? Did he really think it was the best thing
for me? Did he want my power for himself? Did he want me to use my
power only the way he wished it to be used?

Did it really matter? All those motives were twisted, no matter how one
looked at them.

And none of them were "just because he cared about me."
I bent to peer at the hole just a little closer. Not to touch, just to look
and learn.

But as I bent closer, I heard something. A voice. A girl, maybe my own
age.

I'd never had many friends. The few I had made, the relationships never
seemed to last very long.

"Shi. Shi. Shi."

The voice called me. And it sounded exactly as I thought a friend might.

I slowly reached towards the hole.

The book slammed back into place, bruising my hand and closing the hole.

I pulled my hand close to my chest and sent a glare behind me. Father.

Every emotion all at once washed over me. A million things that I wanted to say, that I ought to say, pushed at my mind, but I couldn't put any of them into words and actually speak them.

Father let out a long sigh. There was a quiver to his lip, and for the first time, I realized just how false it truly was.

His hand formed a grasping claw, reaching, stretching out between us.

Something pinched in my mind.

He would use his own powers to take mine away.

Then came a great pulling and tugging—him pulling at those golden strands of power and me tugging back. My head throbbed and a lump rose in my throat.

The strands snapped. And where there had been emotion and questions and heart, there was simply . . .

Emptiness.

He tossed the glowing ball of energy over his shoulder, into a dusty corner. As if it was nothing. As if nothing ever happened. As if he just expected me to be okay with it.

The golden light fizzled out.

I wasn't okay with it.

I still didn't know what to say, but I knew where to start. "Everything you've built here, everything you've given me over these past years is a lie."

He was silent for a long moment before finally whispering, "But it's a beautiful lie, isn't it?"

"No. It's not. You've lied about lots of other things, too. Like how much you loved me. And why you wouldn't let me have friends over. And why I couldn't do the things they did, live a normal life."

"Of course I love you." He seemed wounded that I'd suggested any differently, and for the first time, I recognized the act.

Even though everything inside me was burning, my voice was gentle. "You love what I can do for you. You love the idea of a daughter who fits your idea of perfection."

"Everything I did was to protect you."

This poor fool. He truly believed his own lies. "I believe you believe that."

"You have no idea how dangerous the world is out there." He stabbed a finger at the hole in the bookcase.

"How am I supposed to know? I have no idea whether it actually is or not." I lowered my voice. "And now I can't even trust you."

Anger twisted his face. "You disregard the sacrifices I've made for you like it's nothing."

"This isn't about you," I whispered.

And everything rushed over me at once.

I strode to the corner and picked up the nearly dead ball of energy.

That was alright. I didn't need it.

This something else was coming from deep inside me, and me alone, something no one could ever take away, no matter how hard they tried. I wondered where it had come from. Who or what had put it there. I focused on the hole of golden light that still throbbed deep in the bookcase. Should I? Did I dare? What if it really was as dangerous as he said?

But what if it wasn't?

I grabbed hold of that hole in my mind and pulled.

Horror erupted on Father's face. But not the horror of seeing that his daughter was about to do something dangerous.

The horror of a prized possession slipping out of his grasp.

Books, drywall, and other debris flew everywhere, in slow motion, almost dreamily. I tore apart his reality shred by shred.

For a brief second, I considered building my own. Constructing my own fantasy world where no one could ever hurt me again.

But that wouldn't be reality.

I wanted to experience the world as it really was.

And through all of it, I saw the world outside as it was for the very first time. Not the carefully curated street he'd placed me on, but the truth.

And it was beautiful.

Many of the apartment buildings were run-down and lop-sided. A bent bicycle lay on the sidewalk, and the couple that walked into the dusty bookstore had holes in the knees of their jeans.

But they were talking and laughing. Kids were playing and giggling. It was frightening to stand here with no knowledge of what I was getting into, what my father was trying to hide from me. But it was also freeing.

Perhaps I couldn't have one without the other.

The last shred of Father's reality clung to my hand. I pressed my other hand against a nearby apartment building. It was solid and real and cool under my hand.

I released the shred and stepped forward.

The End.

True Addiction *by Sarfraz Ahmed*

How many times
Do you need to check
The trail of train tracks
On my arms and on my back
Blazing wounds
Punctured deep into my skin.

Blowtorching drops of cocaine
Through my mind
Spiralling alcohol upon my smoke
You lit the fire
You lit the flame.
Fuelled the rocket again and again.

Can't you see I'm riding a bullet?
Flying so high
Too many pills
Have illuminated my mind
But you're just another drug
That I cannot leave behind.

Don't you know
I need all these things and more
I need the all-time high
I need to score
To ride the dragon
And much, much more.

You're just another drug
I cannot let go of
You my true addiction
You are my love.

Leave Me *by Sarfraz Ahmed*

Leave me in the silence
In the corners and the curves
In the echoes of lost souls

Leave me in the solitude
In the loneliness
In the vastness
In the abyss

For in the solitude
You are in my heart all the time
I can feel your eyes penetrate mine.

Leave me behind the clouds
Behind the winged angels
Protected shields

They help to hide the years of hurt
Rejection I know too well
Leave me to walk the path
Between heaven and hell.

What Was Once *by Sarfraz Ahmed*

What was once is no more
Too many closed doors
Constantly holding it in
Not breathing out
Waiting and hoping
That the pain stops
That the anxiety dissolves
Loosens the grip
That it stops taking hold.

Every day
I walk in the shadows
In the cold and dust
Deep down I know
What was once is now lost
Broken and is no more.

Kindling And Kind Heart *by Ndaba Sibanda*

her heart is a hefty,
happy hearth,
a fireplace blazes and plumps
the depths of her interior life
it glows and grows every day
as if fuelled and fanned
by some frantic firewood

The Rose *by Stacy Savage*

You put on a happy face
Everywhere you go.
You tell 'em all you're ok,
But some of them just know
That you are not yourself,
But you swallow your pride.
You show them a mask,
While the pain you hide.
No one understands
Your smile hides a frown
And when you're all alone,
The tears come flowin' down.

The wind carries your secret
And you feel so alone.
You want to reach out
And pick up the phone,
But you don't want to bother
Someone with your woes,
So you thrive on the outside
Like a beautiful rose.
You smile and smile
But you feel the pain
From the thorns of life
And deal with the rain.

Sometimes you have to
Get through the clouds
To get to the sunshine,
And then be proud
Of the person you are,

Even behind the mask.
Dealing with depression
Is a difficult task,
But if you live in darkness,
The sun you'll never know,
And the rose within
Will never get to grow.

Nature's Therapy *by Stacy Savage*

I'm sittin' at Mounds
Listening to the stream.
Before I got here,
I wanted to scream.

My sorrows and troubles
Were getting to me
But as I hear the water,
And the chickadee,

My anxiety rests,
And peace finds its way.
My mind wanders to nature,
Not troubles of the day.

I see threads of silk
Shimmering by the ground
In the patch of sunlight,
As the sun goes down.

I hear the forest echo
The woodpecker's voice.
Instead of breaking down,
I made the right choice

And not let the stress
Begin to take its toll.
Thanks, Mother Nature,
For soothing my soul!

Unshattered *by Stacy Savage*

When I was a kid my sister threw a glass Pepsi bottle in a cooler. The bottle shattered and a piece of glass flew into my arm, leaving behind a tiny scar. So many times, I've looked at that scar and it reminds me of my sister and of happy times of my childhood when we were camping as a family.

She got into a bad car accident at the age of 21 and she went through the windshield and landed on the pavement. She was in a coma and stepped through the pearly gates two months later.

When I see the scar, it could remind me of a sister that's no longer here with me, but time has healed me, and I picked up the broken pieces of my heart and assembled them back together. The pieces are not quite the same but the scar is a beautiful reminder of happy times when two little girls, one brunette, one blonde, had no worries in the world, and represents sisters that will always be together in memories, and in my heart, with a bond–unshattered.

The Masks *by Stacy Savage*

I've always heard you should face your fears. There was one thing that used to bring me a lot of fear. I had a phobia of the comedy/tragedy masks, also known as drama masks, happy/sad masks, theater masks, and smile now cry later masks. It all started when I was around 7 years old. I saw the masks on a wall and a man's voice was chanting my name. I was terrified. It could have been a dream, but it's one I'll never forget.

Over the years since then, I would see the masks occasionally in normal places you would see them, like on tv or in a magazine. I didn't like seeing them but it didn't bring me anxiety until I got with my second ex husband. After I married him, I started seeing them more and more. I remember seeing the masks at work on a poster that was just sitting on the floor and I asked my coworker to turn the poster around. Then I started seeing them in stores, on commercials, on the internet and just random things—even on a birthday cake at a grocery store. It would get my heart pounding.

One day I went to a Goodwill store and was looking at clothes and I decided to go and look at the books, which is something I never do when I go to Goodwill. To my surprise, I saw a book by Sylvia Browne, the psychic that used to be on the Montel Williams show. I picked up the book and I opened the book right to a page that absolutely shocked me. The page was talking about how Sylvia had seen the masks on her wall and how her spirit guide told her that is her life– comedy and tragedy. I bought the book of course. I just couldn't believe that I read that and had opened the book right to that page. It was like I was meant to read it.

My ex-husband was diagnosed bipolar and was a severe alcoholic when I was with him and he was abusive to me. He used to joke and say that he represented the comedy/tragedy masks in my life. He used to joke a lot but would also get very angry at times.

A year before I divorced my ex, I walked into a local flea market. I loved that flea market and had been to it many times. This time was different. Within five minutes I saw the masks in four different areas of the store. After the fourth time, it brought on a full blown panic attack. I was hyperventilating and crying. My legs got really stiff and it was hard to walk. I called my ex at work and asked him to come pick me up and take me home and he did.

A month after that incident my ex was drunk and we got into an argument. He then grabbed me from behind and started choking me. I couldn't breathe and thought I was going to die. He let go of me and there was a big gap on the plank flooring where I was kicking, trying to get away. He also slammed me into the table and against the wall. I stayed in a hotel that night and was grateful to be alive. While I was at the hotel something strange happened. I had this overwhelming feeling that my fear of the masks had disappeared. Could it really be gone? I got my phone out and typed in "comedy/tragedy masks photos"and tons of images of the masks popped up. I began scrolling through them— with no fear whatsoever! The phobia was completely gone! Now that I think about it, I feel like the masks were a warning, and I wasn't paying attention.

I very rarely see the masks on the internet or anywhere— well, except for every day, on my body. A couple months ago, I got a tattoo of the masks—really close to my heart. The tattoo is now a part of me I see in the mirror every day that represents a past I left behind. A past of fear and panic attacks. The masks are now a work of art to me and they symbolize that you don't have to hide behind them, and you can conquer your fears, if you let yourself. Anything is possible.

Mental Illness *by Stephanie Daich*

Mental illness is the thing with tentacles-
That anchors in your heart-
Taking away your joy-
Ripping your soul apart-

Loneliness takes over-
As no one understands-
"Call me," people say-
With empty offers and hands-

The downhearted are left alone-
To rise above the ashes-
Even though others help-
The mental fortitude crashes-

But thankfully, after the struggle-
The light filters in-
Raise your head, fight your demons-
Let the healing begin!

Returning Peace *by Stephanie Daich*

A sliver of light shines through the sky,
Brighter than it's been.
Dark clouds overwhelming
Drowns
Everything within.

Failures illuminated in shadows,
Grinding in the sin.
Hollow feelings spreading
Icy,
Jaded, forsaken.

Killing off the happy times,
Leaching them therein.
Memories good are failing,
Never
Oh, never, again.

Oh, but bring back the light, my strength,
Nourishing pale skin.
Moments sweet returning,
Love
Kicking in.
Joy, pushing out the dreary thoughts,
Incubating a grin.
Hope, spreading as
Good
Feelings begin.

Enriched by inner power,
Defeating the grim.
Calm and peace swelling.
Brightness,
At last, again!

Behind A Mask I Hide *by Stephanie Daich*

-You see me.
I wear a mask designed to deceive.
-You see me.
My life is lies.
I make you believe.
-You see me.
If you knew the real me.
You might grieve.
-You see me.
A heart of stone.
It would make you want to retrieve.
-You see me.
My intentions a web of tangle.
No good I hardly achieve.
-You see me.
But you don't know me.
My goodness, you misconceive.

It's Okay to Let Go *by Teresa Keefer*

When I first laid eyes on that beautiful, brown-eyed baby girl looking up at me on Easter Sunday morning over thirty years ago I didn't realize that one day I would be looking at that now adult daughter and admit to myself she was an addict. I also didn't realize that no matter what I did, I couldn't control that addiction which had taken hold of her and turned her into a person I no longer knew.

It took me a long time to realize that right before my eyes, my daughter who was mother to three beautiful daughters herself, had gone down the path that so many youths have today. But looking at her sitting on the sofa next to her older sister with needle tracks on her arms and tears rolling down both girls' faces, it was painfully obvious. My daughter was a heroin addict.

As a parent, I jumped into gear to 'save' her. Brought her to my house to get her away from the awful drug dealers who were using and exploiting her. Spent hours on the phone trying to get someone, anyone, to give her a bed in a treatment center. Took her to a detox unit and waited for them to call to let me know she could come home. Finally found a Center down south for her to go to. Only for her to call me back a week or so later and say that the place was dirty, had bed bugs, and people were selling drugs. So, she came back to my home. Got a job. And went back to the life I was trying to 'save' her from. I had to send her out on her own because I was not going to have drugs in my house and quite frankly, I needed some peace. Sending her away didn't mean I didn't love her. It just meant I loved myself as well.

There was a time she was rolled out of a car into the entryway of our local hospital by the people who gave her drugs. Helped her use. She was unresponsive. I was out of town when they called. A state away.

And I do not remember any part of the drive back home that morning. I just knew I needed to get to the hospital while I still could.

The nurse reported that the only reason she was still alive was because a doctor getting off duty found her on the cold tiles of the entryway to the emergency room. We sat with her for days. Tried to find treatment for her. I looked at my child sitting in that bed after practically dying and her telling us that there was no helping her. The day I was to have brought her home, she gave me the slip and went to stay with the very people who helped her do drugs. I gave up trying to help but I never stopped loving her.

Less than a year passed and except for the occasional incoherent call or text, I didn't hear a lot from her. Sure, there would be the occasional person reaching out to me and telling me she had posted something negative on social media about any one of us, but those were far and few between. Then there was the night after I ended a call with her because she wasn't making any sense. That night was different. As I sat on my bed later that evening working on a book, I was overcome with the sense of a presence in the room with me. Which isn't unusual for me...but that's a story for another day. When I couldn't ascertain who that soul was, I dismissed it and went about my business. A half hour later, the soul returned even stronger and immediately I spoke her name and felt cold chills all over my body and the feeling of arms around me. I would later find out that she had overdosed and had to be brought back to life. And it wasn't the first time either.

It was close to her birthday when she decided she would try treatment again. I contacted a close friend who helped arrange for her to go out west to a treatment center. We watched her go through security at the airport with her backpack and finally had some hope that this time we would have her back. I visited her on the coast. Watched the daughter I had never seen sober frolic in the water without a care in the world. No needle tracks. No dark circles around her eyes. No pallor to her complexion. I thanked God for this.

Only, she had met a person in treatment who would eventually toss her out of a car on the interstate in a fit of inebriated fury. And she came home. So did he.

The next two years were like a roller coaster. She was clean then she wasn't. She was home then she wasn't. He abused her and turned her into a criminal. When I pointed out that she was not living right, I was thrown out of her apartment while he sat in the bedroom like the lowlife manipulator he was. I went and kept going. Until the day I got the call again.

This time, the diagnosis wasn't an overdose. It was brain damage from repeated blows to the head. Whether they were from her falling down when she overdosed or from her man abusing her, it didn't matter. This was my child and I was going to 'save' her because I love her. We found her a nice apartment. Helped her furnish it. Helped her get a divorce. She got a job and was doing well. Then he got out of jail and dragged her back into the old lifestyle. And she left without a word to her family or her children.

It was then I came to the realization. I had to stop trying to help or fix her. Because the more any of us did, the harder she turned on us when we stopped. Try as we might, we cannot control another human being. We can only control how we respond to others. I quit getting upset and hurt and defensive when she blames me for her addiction problem or her poor choices in life. And now, when people point out to me that she once again has posted her rhetoric on social media I tell them I don't want to know. If they want to believe it, then they don't know me at all. Those who know me know different and all the rest don't matter.

I know this story is just a variation of many others today. The only thing unique about it is the people, places and things that are part of it. Addiction is a harsh reality in today's world and although we try, there are never enough resources and options...and even if there were...the people have to want to take advantage of those resources and options. You can lead a horse to water...right?

My message to other parents of addicts is this...IT'S OKAY TO LET GO...Letting go doesn't mean that I don't love her. I love her unconditionally as a mother is supposed to do. But I love her at a distance. Because I can no longer accept seeing her make the same mistakes over and over again. I can no longer save her. The only person who can do that is herself. And I can't make her want to do that, either. All I can do is pray for her wellbeing. Pray for her health. And pray that someday she will value herself enough to let go of the rope that is holding her in the life she has chosen for herself. That she will understand that it's okay to let go. And to each of you who are experiencing this in your own lives...let go...heal...know peace in your life. It's there as soon as you let go.

Feel To Heal - Standing in My Truth and Trauma
by Terra Chism

This is something I don't talk about publicly but am very open about in private conversations with people when the topic comes up or I know someone else is struggling! As I just hit the three-month mark of my weight loss surgery I also hit the four-month mark of being completely alcohol-free. I didn't drink often but even if I drank one or two times a month, I was going IN on them! I didn't account for the mental battles of giving up food and alcohol at the same time.

The other day I texted my husband, Brandon, "I'm so happy!!!" I have no idea why but I'm just HAPPY! The very next day I picked our youngest up from school and she had a memory from when me and Brandon were separated and was asking me questions about a woman's daughter that she had played with during their brief relationship. I tried to keep my face emotionless and answer her questions. Allow her space to be a kid and process things in her little mind and heart. I'm glad she felt safe to share with me but whew was it hard. I came home and never shared with Brandon the conversation that had taken place on the short ride home but instead curled up in his arms, laid my head on his chest, and said, "I just need a hug because I'm struggling today."

Two extremes from one day to the next. I didn't have food to stuff the problems down and I didn't have alcohol to turn off the noise in my head. I couldn't numb out. I was left to face things head on and sit in my feelings. Can't eat or drink them away. Giving up harmful behaviors and habits and sitting in my truth is HARD as !!!!

But here we are walking out a better life one day at a time! I want to break things off of me for ME, for my kids, and for my grandkids.

To do that means I actually have to sit in the hard moments and acknowledge the hurt, the toxicities of our past, AND the fact that I used food and alcohol to self-medicate. Today, I encourage YOU to dig deep and see what things you can do to better stand in your truth and heal alllllllllll the hidden parts of your journey. You-WE deserve to be truly happy and whole.

Amy *by William Lewis*

It's not easy being an elephant. Out on the plains, with the herd, it's ok, though you have to watch out for the poachers. The lions aren't a problem – they're more wary of us than we are of them. It's not the same in the zoo though. The keepers are kind and our food's provided, but there's never enough space to roam. And I'm not keen on being stared at all day. It's such a relief when the visitors leave. I've been here for fifty years now. I'm the last one here. The others have either died or been taken away. To be honest, it's pretty lonely.

That's not the worst thing, though. The worst thing is that I'm not really an elephant, a great lumbering thing. The truth is, I was born into the wrong body. I know I'm really a butterfly. You can tell by my ears. I can't see them, of course, but I'm sure they're bright colours – iridescent blues, purples and reds. I imagine flapping them and taking off, lifting off the ground. I know that's impossible, though. That's the tragedy of it all, of my life. Well, the second tragedy. The first tragedy is being in here in the first place.

Years ago, I plucked up the courage to tell the others about it, you know, about being a butterfly really and not an elephant.

'Don't be silly, Amy,' they said. 'Just look at you – you're an elephant. Get used to it.'

I never have, though. Some days when there's no-one around I'll go to a quiet corner of our yard and flap my ears as hard as I can. Maybe one day I'll lift up. It's not happened yet, though.

The first time I saw a butterfly I was about four years old. I was transfixed. I gazed, spellbound, at its fragile, delicate beauty.

Up till then I'd known I was in the wrong body, but I didn't know what I was supposed to be. When I first saw one everything fell into place – it made perfect sense, well, to me anyway. It was on one of the bales of hay they attach to the walls of our pen. I watched it for a few moments, then reached my trunk up to it to say hello. Unfortunately, in my excitement, I blew too hard and frightened it away. I didn't make that mistake again. You don't see them very often in here, but I always think they know I'm here and they've come to see me.

I see them in my dreams of course – clouds of bright butterflies flying around me, and I'm up there with them too. Above the ground, above the clouds, under the bright sun. We gambol and play, a shimmering cloud of colour. And I'm one of them. I love those dreams. It's hard waking up from them, back to this heavy body lumbering around. I'm getting tired now. I'll just lie down for a bit. That's better. I can see them fluttering around me. Must be twenty or thirty butterflies.

'Come home Amy,' they say. 'Come home.'

Yes, I will. I'll come home now. I've been away too long. Home to the butterflies. Home to my true self. An elephant no more. I'll flap my wings and fly.

My Life as a Tree *by William Lewis*

My mum told me that when I got to twelve or thirteen I would begin to change, but no-one, least of all me, thought I would turn into a tree. It started one day when my mum suddenly yanked something out of my ear.

'Ow Mum,' I cried, 'what are you doing? That really hurt.'

And it did really hurt. I felt the pain right inside my head.
'Boy,' she said, 'you need to wash more. You've got foliage growing out of your ears.'

And in her hand she showed me a small, green leaf.

'No I haven't,' I said. 'No-one has leaves in their ears.'

But I did wonder whether it had come from me.

Over the next few weeks I began to sprout more leaves, little twigs grew from my head and body, and from them these delicate, oval, unmistakably green leaves. To say I was worried would be an understatement, yet at the same time I felt a sense of peace, a contentment. Something about it felt right for me. I became much taller, my knees stiffer, my legs thicker, and my skin became a hard, brown, coarse carapace. Much the same happened to my arms, with small branches growing from them, and again a profusion of leaves. My parents were horrified, but I felt a strange sense of calm inside myself. School became very difficult. Some threw stones at me.

'Hey, Tree Boy, keep away from us. We don't want your mange.'

One boy tried to carve his initials on my back. As I grew even taller some kids tried to climb me. Perhaps I wouldn't have minded if they'd asked first, but I think they now saw me as a thing, rather than a person. It was understandable. I certainly didn't look like a person. You'd have struggled to make out my face. I was still me inside, though a different kind of me who I'd not really come to terms with yet.

By now I couldn't even get into our home, and spent my nights standing in the garden. The nights were very peaceful, no-one bothered me. Anyway, I knew I couldn't stay there, so one night I set off for the forest. It didn't feel like I was leaving home. It felt like I was going home.

I've been here for five years now. It's a good place, this glade, here with Henry, Alice, David and Colin, Duncan and Nicole. Sometimes on a quiet moonlit evening we'll change places, move around a bit just for a change of scene. No-one ever notices. I thought Colin was a bit dull at first, but he really makes me laugh now. Nicole is very elegant. She trained as a ballet dancer, but she says she doesn't miss it. Well not much. She's a silver birch. I love the way she sways with the wind, the way the light moves on her: she's still a dancer. My best friend is Annette. She was born in Putney, but now she's a chaffinch. She sings to me. She built a nest in my upper branches. I wrap my arms around it to hold it, to keep her chicks safe when the wind blows.

A family came here the other day. I thought they were going to join us, but it was just for a picnic.

I heard one of them say, 'What a lovely place here. We must enjoy it before the loggers come.'

I wasn't sure what they meant by that, but I didn't like the sound of it. And I was right. I never thought I'd end up as bits of flatpack. And I miss them: Henry, Alice, David, Colin, Duncan. And Nicole's dancing. They were good days. The saws were brutal. I often wonder what happened to Annette.

First Prize Scar *by Zaneta Varnado Johns*

Boldly she reveals her tummy's scar
The distinct mark that carried her thus far
Marvelous that she is not ashamed
Of the wound required to heal her pain

That scar portrays a warrior's strength
Her will to live—tested at great lengths
This teen now thrives in whatever she does
Her light reveals God's pure grace and love

Most people shield their scars from view
Her confident spirit is daring and true
Fearless she is—completely unfazed
Awarded first prize for winning life's race

A Message for the Scarred from The Universe
by ChatGPT

Scars are a testament
To the battles we've fought
A reminder of the pain
That we've bravely overcome
Some scars are visible
A mark upon the skin
A constant reminder
Of where we've been
Other scars are hidden
Deep within our hearts
A wound that may have healed
But never truly parts
But no matter where they are
These scars are a part of us
A symbol of our strength
A testament to trust
For every scar we bear
Is a story to be told
Of the struggles we've faced
And the stories yet to unfold
So let your scars be a reminder
Of all that you have been through
And know that you are braver
Than anyone knew

About The Authors

Big Sal - Master of Holorime, check the diction and count the rhymes. bigsalpoetryblog.wixsite.com/bigsalpoetry

Bryan Franco is a gay, Jewish poet from Brunswick, Maine. He competed with the Portland, Maine Rhythmic Cypher slam team in the 2014 National Poetry Slam in Oakland, California. He has been published in the US, Australia, England, India, Ireland, and Scotland and has featured for poetry events in the US, Canada, England, Ireland, and Scotland. He was a finalist in the 2022 NAMI NJ Dara Axelrod Expressive Arts Poetry Contest. He hosts Café Generalissimo Open Mic, is a member of the Beardo Bards of the Bardo poetry troupe, workshop facilitator, painter, sculptor, gardener, and culinary genius. His book "Everything I Think Is All in My Mind" was published in 2021 by Read Or Green Books.

Chuck Kellum - His poem, "Living" is in the Indiana INverse online poetry archive. "The Person That You Are" was performed in the Stage 1 Dance Academy *Words in Motion* event March 2023. "The Dreams of a Woman or Man" was displayed September - October 2021 in the *Dreamscape & Belief* exhibit at Nickel Plate Arts. Chuck grew up on a Hoosier farm and began making poetry while a senior in college studying engineering. He made about 120 poems in the course of a dozen years before getting married, but then was too busy after that with work and family. His making of poems on a somewhat frequent basis resumed in 2009 after his kids were grown and he was no longer working full time. Poems of his have been included in several small journals and anthologies. He enjoys ongoing affiliation with other poets in various ways, including the "ModPo" online study community, the Noble Poets poetry group, and Poetry Society of Indiana.

Clara Klein has been a freelance writer of inspirational poetry and prose for over 30 years. Her focus is writing about real world experiences from her own philosophical perspective. She has been published in books, anthologies, and literary and spiritual journals.

Clay Octobre

Colleen Wells' work has appeared in Gyroscope Review, Ravensperch, and The Potomac Review. She is the author of Dinner With Doppelgangers – A True Story of Madness and Recovery and Animal Magnetism – A Poetry Chapbook.

D.A. Cairns – Heavy metal lover and cricket tragic, D.A. Cairns lives on the south coast of News South Wales. He works as a freelance writer, has had over 90 short stories published, and has authored seven novels, plus a superficial and unscientific memoir, I Used to be an Animal Lover. His latest novel is the second book in the Callumron series, The Sorcerer's Tusk. You may like to visit his website dacairns.com.au

Diana Humphrey lives in southwest England in an area of outstanding natural beauty, teeming with artists, craftsmen, poets, and writers of all kinds. They all stimulate her to keep attending classes, festivals, readings, and publishing.

EB Hills

Elizabeth Cox is a poet and co-author of *Remember When*. She lives in Marion, Indiana with her husband Chris and their exotic fish. Elizabeth loves to garden, spend time with her family, workout with her best friend, and go to rummage sales.

Isabella St. Kim – A voice to the voiceless since 1997. Published Recognize the Naked Truth. Available on Amazon. Email izzybelle724@gmail.com.

Jason Bayliss

Jessica Oakwood is a mental health writer who has previously contributed to various anthologies such as *Spectrum* and *Our Stories to Tell*. She has an MA in Creative Writing and an undergraduate degree in English Literature.

John Ganshaw – At the age of 53 and after 31 years in banking it was time for John to retire and follow his dream of owning a hotel in Southeast Asia. This led to many new experiences enabling John to see the world through a different lens, leading him to write his story through essays, poetry, and a yet unpublished memoir. Nothing is as it seems. There is hope, truth, and adventure in life, all leading to stories that need to be written and told.

Julie A. Dickson is a poet who loves cats, is a pushcart nominee, past poetry board member, and advocates for captive elephants. Her poetry appears in various journals and on Amazon.

Karuna Mistry is a British writer of Indian ethnicity. He regularly publishes poetry in Mckinley Publishing Hub, Open Door, and Sweetycat Press. Sometimes, he's even been paid for his poetry. Karuna is currently working on his debut poetry book. As well as poetry, drawing and blogging, his creativity includes magazine editorship, photography, and design – his occupation by day is higher education marketing. Follow @Karunamistrypoetry on Instagram.

Kathy Chaffin Gerstorff is a poet, indie author, and creative entrepreneur. She started the Indie Authors Association to help independent authors and aspiring writers with the business side of writing. Kathy loves to write and publish books to help good causes. She has contributed to and published several anthologies including *Break The Cycle* series, *Naturally Yours*, *Remember When*, *Nature Matters*, and *Who Told You That*. Kathy hosts the [BOOKENDS] podcast, co-hosts the Hoosier Indie Authors Book Fair, and she is the Contest Director for Poetry Society of Indiana. When Kathy is not writing, publishing, or helping indie authors, you can find her reading, swimming, walking, gardening, or crafting—currently it's making bookends. You can see what Kathy is up to and join the indie authors family by visiting writerkat.com.

Leland P. Gamson - After retiring from the VA and U.S. Army, he is focusing on writing stories for young people. He is a member of the American Academy of American Poets. His books can be found on his website at lelandpgamson.com.

Dr. Lori Goss-Reaves is a professor of social work at Indiana Wesleyan University and an advocate for veterans, Gold Star Families, and individuals with special needs. Through her work as a Licensed Clinical Social Worker, Dr. Goss-Reaves inspires families to tell their own stories of resilience, hope, and love. Lori recently wrote a book about her father, Navy Corpsman Larry Jo Goss, who was killed in action during the Vietnam War, while attempting to save the life of a wounded Marine. Her book, Kiss Lori For Me, was the #1 New Release on Amazon for thirty-eight days, holding the spot in four different categories. Her book climbed to the #2 Best Seller in the category of Military Families and #2 Best Seller on Kindle. Lori is a gifted speaker who shares her father's legacy of love and her mother's undying love with audiences throughout the United States. Her author talks/book signings spotlight Vietnam Veterans who share their own stories at these events.

Lori is married to syndicated cartoonist Eric Reaves, who draws the *Hi and Lois* comic strip. Lori and Eric reside in Indiana, where they raised their five children. Five grandchildren now fill their lives with joy. To book Lori to speak please contact her at lorireaves@me.com or visit kissloriforme.com.

Marcia Durant was born in Indiana and grew up in a small Farming community located in northern Madison county. Since Marcia was a small child she has had a compassion for animals in need and a love of photography as well as the outdoors. She has been drawn to writing short stories and poetry since grade school, poetry being her favorite. Marcia wrote short fictional stories while in high school for the "Tartan" her school's literary publication. She also enjoyed working on the Yearbook staff in junior high through 12th grade. Poetry has become her hobby and favorite release. Marcia has two grown children and has lived on a farm in Pendleton for 33+ years where she owned and operated an in-home state licensed child care since 1984. Her poetry and essays have been published in the Indiana Voice Journal, as well as various other publications and in numerous poetry anthologies available on Amazon and Lulu press. She won an honorable mention in the State Poetry competition among thousands of entrants.

Marj O'Neill-Butler, a resident of Miami Beach, Florida, is the Regional Rep for the Dramatists Guild – Florida Region. She is also a member of the New Play Exchange, Honor Roll and the International Center for Women Playwrights. Her work has been seen in 32 states, the District of Columbia, Canada, Great Britain, Scotland, Australia, Malaysia, Hong Kong and Seoul, S. Korea. She has had 59 different plays produced in multiple theatres, numerous readings and of course, many rejections. A published playwright and mother of two grown sons, Marj is a proud member of Actors Equity and SAG-AFTRA.

Michael "Maik" Strosahl was born and raised in Moline, Illinois, just blocks from the Mississippi River. He has written poetry since youth, but it was mainly after moving to Indiana and participating in a poetry reading on a dare that he became involved in the Indiana poetry scene, becoming a part of what is now known as the Poetry Society of Indiana and traveling the state in search of the small groups that met in living-rooms, upstairs library groups and coffee houses, even starting groups in communities where he found none. From each he grew, and hopes he helped others to try new things with their talent. He served the PSI as Membership Chair and eventually as President. In 2018, he relocated to Jefferson City, MO, beginning his search anew for kindred spirits to inspire and draw energy from. He currently co-hosts a monthly critiquing group in the capital city. Maik's work has appeared in *The Tipton Poetry Journal, The Last Stanza Journal, Bards Against Hunger* projects, *The Polk Street Review*, PSI projects, several projects for *Poetry Contests for a Cause*, and online at *Project Agent Orange, Our Day's Encounter, Indiana Voice Journal, Poetry Super Highway*—plus on several city buses and in a museum. He also does a weekly blog post for *Moristotle & Company* called "Hobnobbing with the Philosophers." Maik's poem *Wharton Creek* appeared previously in his blog series on *Moristotle & Company*.

Mikayla Cyr is a Maine native who collects tattoos, music paraphernalia, and has been putting her feelings onto paper since 2003. She also loves nature, animals, and concerts.

Ndaba Sibanda is a Bulawayo-born poet, novelist and nonfiction writer who has authored twenty-eight published books of various genres and persuasions and co-authored more than 100 published books. Some of Ndaba`s works are found or forthcoming in *Page & Spine, Piker Press, Scarlet Leaf Review, Universidad Complutense de Madrid, the Pangolin Review, Kalahari Review, Botsotso, The Ofi Press Magazine, Hawaii Pacific Review, Deltona Howl, The song is, JONAH magazine, Saraba Magazine, Poetry Potion, Saraba Magazine, The Borfski Press, East Coast Literary Review* and *Whispering Prairie Press.* Sibanda has received the following nominations: the national arts merit awards (NAMA), the *Mary Ballard Poetry Chapbook Prize*, the *Best of the Net Prose* and the *Pushcart Prize.*
pagespineficshowcase.com/ndaba-sibanda.html
ndabasibanda.wordpress.com/2017/03/26/first-blog-post/

Noel Arzola (Jessica Grissom) lives in a small Texas town with her husband and their rainbow baby. Her passions include books, writing, chocolate, jewelry, traveling, and tea. She obtained an MBA from Dallas Baptist University and worked in the business industry for eighteen years. Her story, Ascensión, was published in the creative writing journal, The Image, at Southwestern Assemblies of God University. In her spare time, she records a podcast, The More You Know, that focuses on honest discussions and practical tips for living.
anchor.fm/jessica-n-grissom

Pratibha Savani is a UK poet and artist. She works in education, is a busy mum and enjoys yoga, reading and science fiction. Her debut book, Tangles + Knots, published in October 2020, uniquely combines her art and writing with mindfulness and wellbeing themes. She is featured in anthologies by Prolific Pulse Press LLC, McKinley Publishing Hub and Sweetycat Press as well as in publications by Open Door Poetry Magazine and Fine Lines. Pratibha is a creative soul, inspired by the cosmos, nature and spirituality and likes to defy the rules with her inventive expressions on instagram and facebook as @pratibhapoetryart.

Rachel Leitch discovered the book of writing when she was seven. She's been turning pages ever since! She lives her own adventure in northern Indiana, with her parents, three sisters, two brothers, and a dog who thinks he's the hero of her story. She writes young adult historical fiction with a dash of adventure or a spark of magic.

When Rachel's not hidden away penning young adult fiction, she's trying to fit all her reads on her shelf in a somewhat organized manner, rambling through history, daydreaming at the piano, or teaching students to be just as bookish as she is. In all her adventures, she learns how to shine brighter for the Father of Lights. Join the adventure (and get a free short story) at racheljleitch.com or on Instagram at @racheljleitchauthor.

Sarfraz Ahmed is a world acknowledged writer and Amazon bestseller who achieved success globally as a poet. His published books include poetry debut *Eighty-Four Pins – Poetry Collection* (June 2020, 2022) and *My Teacher's an Alien!* (November 2020). *Two Hearts – A Journey into Heartfelt Poetry* (February 2021) with Annette Tarpley and *Stab the Pomegranate – Collective Poetry* (August 2021). The second edition of *Eighty-Four Pins – Poetry Collection* was published in February 2022, followed by the global release of *The Gift of Poetry* (June 2022) specially dedicated to all his supporters. Sarfraz is an administrator of one of the largest poetry groups on Facebook, 'The Passion of Poetry' and has a following on Instagram #sarfrazahmedpoet. In May 2021 he was recognized as a World Contributor Poet, recognised for his contribution to poetry by Administrators, Poetry and Literature World Vision. We can find him at open mic events, where he has shared his poetry globally.

Stacy Savage has published several anthologies that benefited multiple charities. Her work has been published in numerous publications, including *Birds and Blooms*, *Ideals* magazine, *Asian Geographic*, and *Tipton Poetry Journal*. She was a judge twice in the former *Best Books of Indiana* competition that was held by the Indiana State Library. She resides in Yorktown, Indiana and has two adult children.

Stephanie Daich carries you to the land of stories. Publications include *Making Connections*, *Youth Imaginations*, *Chicken Soup for the Soul: Kindness Matters*, and others.
stephdaich3.wixsite.com/phoenix-z-publishing

Teresa Keefer was chosen by her adoptive parents in Warsaw, Indiana and has remained in Indiana all her life. She currently resides in rural Indiana with a menagerie of dogs, cats and goats after a family of greedy raccoons ate all her chickens on a hot Saturday night. She has three beautiful adult daughters and seven fantastic grandchildren who all live a hop, skip and a jump away from her. A life-long lover of books, Teresa learned to read at the age of four and has been an avid reader ever since she won her community's bookmobile reading contest and got to ride the library float in the Canal Days parade in Wabash, Indiana. As an adult, she was encouraged by her know-it-all best friend to write a book after he gave her a book idea and she cranked out three chapters the first day. After writing her first full-length novel—*Coming Home*—she got disappointed in all the canned rejection letters, so she went in search of another option and learned about self-publishing. *Coming Home* is a sweet, contemporary romance which takes place in a fictional town called Possum Creek and was published in February 2012. Since then, there have been two additional *Possum Creek* novels along with over twenty more novels including the Amazon best-selling, steamy, paranormal thriller *Vincent-Blood Retribution*, the first in her New Orleans vampire series. She has also contributed to six anthologies, the most recent being *Hope Harbor* which all proceeds go to an organization which supports the rescue and rehabilitation of victims of child sex trafficking. Holding an MBA from Indiana Institute of Technology, she has spent the last 30 years in the human resources profession. In her spare time—what little there is—she can be found doing a variety of crafts, cooking, studying the paranormal, making organic remedies, and barefoot gardening. Her bucket list is quite extensive, and she is determined to mark off every item—as she adds two more for each one accomplished.

Terra Chism – Warrior for Christ, wife, mother, grandmother, entrepreneur, author, speaker, and fitness/health enthusiast. terrachism.com, communityunitynetwork.org

William Lewis - Writing has always been a strong part of William Lewis's life, from professional reports to book reviews, poetry and song lyrics for bands he has performed with. Four years ago he discovered Flash Fiction, which has opened up for him a new avenue of creativity. He particularly enjoys the economy and possibilities of the short form, and has now had several stories published by online magazines. Some of his stories are light and humorous, others are darker. He particularly enjoys reading his stories aloud. He has read his stories on a Gloucestershire local radio station and, during 2022, at several Gloucestershire arts centres. Many of his stories have strong visual elements, and a number of them are being used as source material for a group of artists in northern Germany, leading to the production of a book with text in English and German.

Zaneta Varnado Johns, aka Zan Johns, is a Pushcart Nominee in Poetry and 4-time bestselling author of *Poetic Forecast* (2020) and *After the Rainbow* (2022). Johns is a contributing author in the Women Speakers Association's #1 international bestsellers *Voices of the 21st Century* (2021, 2022, 2023). Her poems are featured as the Dedication page in these collaborative books.

Johns co-edited Social Justice Inks anthology (2022) with publisher and poet Lisa Tomey-Zonneveld. She serves as an editor for the *Fine Lines Literary Journal* and administrator for the *Passion of Poetry*, a revered online platform for emerging and esteemed poets. Her poems appear in over fifty anthologies and international literary publications. Believing that every word shared is an opportunity to love, Johns' writing offers hope as she stirs the reader's consciousness about life and living.

Johns is a retired human resources leader who spent her twenty-nine-year career at the University of Colorado. She was recognized in 2007 as one of the University of Colorado's Women Who Make a Difference. Johns resides in Westminster, Colorado, USA. zanexpressions.com

Resources

National Alliance on Mental Illness (NAMI) - Call or text the NAMI Helpline at 800-950-6264 or chat with them by texting "HelpLine" to 62640, Monday - Friday 10 a.m. - 10 p.m. Eastern Standard Time. NAMI is the nation's largest grassroots mental health organization dedicated to building better lives for millions of Americans affected by mental illness. nami.org

988 Suicide and Crisis Lifeline - Call or text 988. By calling or texting 988, you'll connect with mental health professionals with the 988 Suicide and Crisis Lifeline, formerly known as the National Suicide Prevention Lifeline. Veterans can press "1" after dialing 988 to connect directly to the Veterans Crisis Lifeline which serves our nation's Veterans, service members, National Guard and Reserve members, and those who support them. Crisis counselors listen empathetically and without judgment. Your crisis counselor will work to ensure that you feel safe and help identify options and information about mental health services in your area. 988 is the new, shorter phone number that will make it easier for people to access mental health crisis services. Crisis Text Line – Text HOME to 741-741 to connect with a trained crisis counselor to receive free, 24/7 crisis support via text message. 988lifeline.org

National Domestic Violence Hotline – Call 800-799-SAFE (7233) Trained expert advocates are available 24/7 to provide confidential support to anyone experiencing domestic violence or seeking resources and information. Help is available in Spanish and other languages.

National Sexual Assault Hotline – Call 800-656-HOPE (4673)
Connect with a trained staff member from a sexual assault service provider in your area that offers access to a range of free services. Crisis chat support is available at hotline.rainn.org. Free help, 24/7.

Authors & Books

Dr. Henry Cloud & Dr. Dan Allender helped me immensely on my healing journey. I discovered them during a *Day of Healing* conference at the Honeywell Center in Wabash, Indiana. I highly recommend their books and workshops. I am also a big fan of the late Louise Hay. Her book *You Can Heal Your Life* helped me learn the power of words to heal my mind, body, and spirit. ~ *Kathy Chaffin-Gerstorff*

What books or other resources have helped you? Email kathy@indieauthorsassociation.com to add it to our *SCARS* Resource list at scarspoetrybook.com.

Made in the USA
Middletown, DE
30 March 2023

27959141R00128